Soccer Mindset:

A Step-by-Step Guide on How to Outsmart Your Opponents and Improve Your Mentality

Dylan Joseph

Soccer Mindset:
A Step-by-Step Guide on How to Outsmart Your Opponents and
Improve Your Mentality

By: Dylan Joseph

WAIT!

Wouldn't it be nice to have an easy 1-page checklist of the steps to master your morning? Need the tasks to do to make sure you have a terrific start to your day? Well, here is your chance!

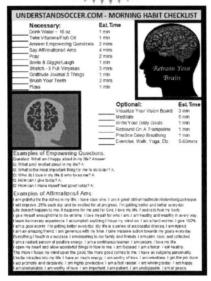

Go to this Link for an **Instant** 1-Page Printout:
UnderstandSoccer.com/free-printout

This FREE checklist is simply a "Thank You" for purchasing this book. This 1-page checklist will ensure that you take advantage of every morning to bring you closer to becoming the best soccer player you can be!

Table of Contents

Dedication

This book is dedicated to you, the soccer player, who cares enough about your success that you are willing to read a book to improve your mentality, mindset, and attitude. Learning is exceptionally noble and speaks volumes to the person you are.

Also, this book is dedicated to Carol S. Dweck, Tony Robbins, Richard Carlson, Jim Rohn, Earl Nightingale, & Jesus Christ who have helped me develop my mindset and pushed me to know the importance of hard work. Their guidance in what mindsets are most beneficial has been huge in helping me become a better person. For them, I am very thankful.

Preface

Having a mentally tough mindset can be the difference from average performances and lifting the trophy at the end of the season. Because all action originates in your mind, if you can train your mind to succeed, the actions and results you want will follow. This book gives you the tips, tricks, tweaks, and techniques to become mentally strong, open to feedback, and avoid the one mindset that holds most people back.

INDIVIDUAL SOCCER PLAYER'S PYRAMID

If you are looking to improve your skills, your child's confidence, or your players' abilities, it is essential to understand where this book fits into the bigger picture of developing a soccer player. In the image, you can see the most critical field-specific skills to work on are at the base of the Individual Soccer Player's Pyramid. The pyramid is a quality outline that you can use to improve an individual soccer player's game. All the elements in the pyramid and the items surrounding it play a meaningful part in becoming a better player, but certain skills should be read and mastered first before moving to the others.

You will notice that passing and receiving is at the foundation of the pyramid because if you can receive a pass and make a pass in soccer, you will be a useful teammate. Though you may not be the one that is consistently scoring, the person that is dispossessing the other team, or the player that can dribble through several opponents, you will have the fundamental tools needed to play the sport and contribute to your team.

As you move one layer up, you find yourself with a decision to make on how to progress. Specifically, the pyramid is created with you in mind because each soccer player and each soccer position has different needs. Therefore, your choice regarding which path to take first is dictated by the position you play and more importantly, by the position that you want to play.

In soccer and life, just because you are in a particular spot, position, or even a job, it does not mean that you have to stay there forever if that is not your choice. However, it is not recommended to refuse playing a position if you are not in the exact role you want. It takes time to develop the skills that will allow you to make a shift from one position to another.

If you want to become a forward, then consider starting your route on the second layer of the pyramid with shooting and finishing. As your abilities to shoot increase, your coach will notice your new finishing skills and will be more likely to move you up the field if you are not a forward already. Be sure to communicate to the coach that you desire to be moved up the field to a more offensive position, which will increase your chances, as well. If you are already a forward, then dive deep into this topic to ensure you become the leading scorer; first on your team, and then in the entire league. Notice that shooting and finishing is considered less critical than passing and receiving because you have to pass the ball up the field before you can take a shot on net.

Otherwise, you can start by progressing to dribbling & foot skills from passing & receiving because the proper technique is crucial to dribble the ball well. It is often necessary for a soccer player to use a skill to protect the ball from the other team or to advance the ball up the field to place their team in a favorable situation to score. The selection of this route is often taken first by midfielders and occasionally by forwards.

Defending is another option of how you can proceed from passing and receiving. Being able to keep the other team off the scoreboard is not an easy task. Developing a defender's mindset, learning which way to push a forward, understanding how to position your body, knowing when to foul, and using the correct form for headers is critical to a defender on the back line looking to prevent goals.

Finish all three areas in the second layer of the pyramid before progressing up the pyramid. Dribbling and defending the ball (not just shooting) are useful for an attacker, shooting and defending (not just dribbling) are helpful for a midfielder, while shooting and dribbling (not just defending) are helpful for a defender. Having a well-rounded knowledge of the skills needed for the different positions is important for all soccer players. It is especially essential for those soccer players looking to change positions in the future. Shooting and finishing, dribbling and foot skills, and defending are oftentimes more beneficial for soccer players to learn first than the next tier of the pyramid, so focus on these before spending time on areas higher up in the pyramid. In addition, reading about each of these areas will help you to understand what your opponent wants to do as well.

Once you have improved your skills in the first and second tiers of the pyramid, move up to fitness. As you practice everything below this category on the pyramid, your fitness and strength will naturally increase. It is difficult to go through a passing/dribbling/finishing drill for a few minutes without being out of breath. Performing technical drills allows soccer players to increase their fitness naturally. This reduces the need to focus exclusively on running for fitness. Coming from a soccer player and trainer (i.e., someone with a view from both sides), I know that constantly focusing on running is not as fulfilling and does not create long-lasting improvements, whereas emphasizing shooting capabilities, foot skills, and defending knowledge creates long-lasting change. Often, coaches who focus on running their players in practice are also coaches who want to improve their team but have limited knowledge of many of the soccer-specific topics that would quickly increase their players' abilities. Not only does fitness in soccer include your endurance; it also addresses your ability to run with agility and speed, develop strength and power, while improving your flexibility through stretching to become a well-rounded soccer player.

Similar to the tier below it, you should focus on the fitness areas that will help you specifically, while keeping all of the topics in mind. For example, you may be a smaller soccer player who could use some size. In this case, you should emphasize weight training so that you can gain the muscle needed to avoid being pushed off the ball. However, you should still stretch before and after a lifting workout or soccer practice/game to ensure that you stay limber and flexible to recover quickly and avoid injuries.

Maybe you are a soccer player in your 20s, 30s, or 40s. Then, emphasizing your flexibility and practicing a bit of yoga would do a world of good to ensure you keep playing soccer for many more years. However, doing a few sets of push-ups, pull-ups, squats, lunges, sit-ups, etc. per week will help you maintain or gain a desirable physique.

Furthermore, you could be in the prime of your career in high school, college, or at the pro level, which means that obtaining the speed and endurance needed to run for 90+ minutes is the most essential key to continue pursuing your soccer aspirations.

Finally, we travel to the top of the pyramid which involves tryouts. Though tryouts occur only one to two times per year, they have a huge impact on whether you make the team you want to join or get left out of the lineup. Tryouts can cause intense nerves if you do not know the keys to making sure that you stand out and are very confident from the start.

If you have not read the *Understand Soccer* series book, *Soccer Training*, it is highly recommended that you do to gain the general knowledge of crucial topics within the areas of the pyramid. Picking up a copy of the book will act as a good gauge to see how much you know about each topic, which will help determine if a book later in the series written about a specific subject in the soccer pyramid will be beneficial for you.

The last portion of the pyramid are the areas that surround the pyramid. Though these are not skills and topics that can be addressed by your physical abilities, they each play key roles in rounding out a complete soccer player. For example, having a supportive parent/guardian or two is beneficial for transporting the child to games, providing the equipment needed, the fees for the team, expenses for individual training, and encouragement. Having a quality coach whose teachings and drills help the individual learn how their performance and skills fit into the team's big picture helps a lot too.

Sleeping enough is critical to having energy in practices and on game days, in addition to recovering from training and games. Appropriate soccer nutrition will increase a soccer player's energy and endurance, help them achieve the ideal physique, and significantly aid in their recovery. Understanding soccer positions will help you determine if a specific role is well-suited for your skills. It is important to know that there are additional types of specific positions—not just forwards, midfielders, and defenders. A former or current professional player in the same position as you can provide guidance on the requirements to effectively play that position.

Finally, you must develop a mindset that will leave you unshakable. This mindset will help you prepare for game situations, learn how to deal with other players, and be mentally tough enough to not worry about circumstances that you cannot control, such as the type of field you play on, the officiating, or the weather.

The pyramid is a great visual aid to consider when choosing what areas to focus on next as a soccer player, coach, or parent. However, remember that a team's pyramid may look slightly different based on which tactics the players can handle and which approach the coach decides to use for games. Now that you know where this book plays into the bigger picture, let us begin.

Remember that if there are any words or terms whose meaning you are unsure of; you can feel free to reference the glossary at the back of the book. **Finally, if you enjoy this book, please leave a review on Amazon letting me know.**

Chapter 1

Growth Mindset vs. Fixed Mindset

Philosopher William James has stated, "The greatest discovery of my generation is that a human being can alter his life by altering his *attitudes*." Essentially, a person's mindset as they experience events, as well as how they reflect upon them afterward, is a key indicator of how quickly that person will grow. One of the best things to help you grow in in soccer and life is understanding the difference between a fixed mindset and a growth mindset.

The fixed mindset is that of someone who believes their basic qualities of intelligence, talent, humor, athletic ability, etc. are fixed traits. Those with fixed mindsets find areas where they can show how great they are versus looking for opportunities that are humbling and will allow them to grow. Also, people with fixed mindsets tend to rely on talent for their success. For example, a fixed mindset for a soccer player is believing they have a fixed trait about how hard they can shoot a soccer ball.

On the other hand, a person with a growth mindset knows that their basic qualities of intelligence, talent, humor, athletic ability, etc. are just abilities they have

developed over time, using knowledge and hard work. People with growth mindsets look for opportunities slightly outside their comfort zone to grow from the new experiences. They understand certain people are more suited for certain jobs, roles, or positions in life. They know that with focused effort, they can change their basic qualities and rely on hard work, along with continuous learning to ensure a life of growth. For example, a growth mindset for a soccer player is believing they can improve how hard they can shoot by lifting weights to gain muscle, reading about what is good shooting form, finding a trainer to guide them on abilities, and practicing to become a much more powerful shooter.

Generally, people are not in a 100% fixed mindset or a 100% growth mindset. They are somewhere between these two ends of the spectrum. The trick is to direct yourself towards the growth mindset. Here are some examples of fixed mindset (FM) phrases and growth mindset (GM) phrases:

FM: I am a failure because I did not do well in a soccer game.
GM: I may have failed in the game but if I work harder, I will become better and succeed next time.

FM: I am doing this because I want to look smart.
GM: I am doing this because I want a challenge.

FM: I did well because I am talented.

GM: I did well because I am a hard worker, and I am applying what I am learning.

FM: They did well because they were lucky.

GM: They did well because they made their own luck.

A fault with the human mind is the need to appear consistent. Many people value consistency over growth and learning what is right. Take a minute and think about a relative you have—maybe an aunt or uncle who is always telling everyone "how it really is." Possibly, you have a parent who gets into arguments and occasional shouting matches when someone disagrees with them. Maybe you have a son or daughter who does not like to attempt new things but cannot verbalize and tell you why, other than because "they just don't like trying new things." People like this want to appear consistent in everything they do, they avoid new experiences outside their comfort zone, and they find fault in others without realizing they have many faults themselves. These are the same people who need to look smart in the short-run, which almost always ensures they do not look smart in the long-run.

Remember that anyone can change, but often it is the person with a growth mindset who will. Personally, I used to have a fixed mindset. After reading many books, I realized it was holding me back tremendously. Malcolm Gladwell, a three-time New York Best-Selling author in the field of personal development, points out that our society prefers effortless successes than a person having to struggle to succeed. This is so true but also very sad because talent is not something to control but learning and working hard are controllable.

An example of a person who fell into the trap of a fixed mindset is Freddy Adu. Adu made world news when he was DC United's first pick in the MLS Super Draft in 2004. Amazingly, he was only 14 years old. The attacking midfielder soon was compared to Pelé, one of the greatest soccer players of all-time. Yes, before Adu even set foot on a professional field, he was already receiving the hype reserved only for those players who had already proven themselves. Sadly, Adu did not live up to many Americans' hopes for a world-class soccer player whom we could call our own. He played for 12 clubs in eight different countries over his career and made little difference at each of the clubs he joined.

His early successes, before the age of 14, were often said to come from his natural abilities. The problem was that he could not improve his natural abilities. Those were things he either had or did not have. The constant praise during Adu's childhood likely resulted in a very fixed mindset. Carol S. Dweck, Ph.D. in her famous book, *Mindset*, revealed that when children are praised for their intelligence and natural abilities rather than for their ability to work hard, their motivation to take on challenges drops and their performances on later tasks diminishes significantly. If you have a son or daughter and want to ensure they grow up without the limiting beliefs that a person with a fixed mindset has, consider grabbing the *Understand Soccer* series book, *Soccer Parenting,* for a step-by-step guide on growing your child's self-esteem and abilities in soccer and in life.

Even if you make mistakes, remind yourself to distinguish the difference between learning and failing. **Failing is when you mess up and give up without learning.** Many of the most successful people in the world have made more mistakes than anyone else, but they never stopped working toward their dreams. Remember, you have only truly failed once you have given up.

YouTube: If you would like to see a video on the difference between the growth and fixed mindset, then watch the *Understand Soccer* YouTube video: Growth vs. Fixed Mindset.

Chapter 2

Challenging vs. Threatening

Imagine you have two games this upcoming weekend. Before the first game, your parent tells you, "This game will be a great challenge. It will test what you are made of and will take lots of effort. I am excited for you to compete tomorrow." Come game time, you are alert and excited to play. Your body is releasing adrenaline, and you are ready to rock! You do your best and contribute to your team's victory. Terrific!

Before the second game that weekend, the same parent has another conversation with you. They say, "The other team is coming for your team. Even though you guys were in first place all season, your opponent tomorrow could really threaten your team's chance of winning the championship." Just before the start of the game, you seem nervous and tense. Your body is releasing the stress hormone cortisol and you want to be anywhere but on the field.

When confronted with the same game of soccer against two teams that were relatively similar in talent, you responded differently based on conversations you had before each game. The conversation before the first game, you were told, "The game will be a great challenge. It will test what you are made of and will take lots of effort. I am excited for you in the competition tomorrow." However, before the second game, your parent stated, "The other team is coming for your team. Even though you guys were in first place all season, your opponent tomorrow could really threaten your team's chance of winning the championship."

At first glance, these seem like two very similar conversations with your parent who was showing support and love. With both conversations, your parent believed they were helping steer you towards victory. However, if you look a little deeper, you will notice each of the talks changed how you were feeling on the field to start the game. Though there are more factors that can play a role like your personality and views on how things work, notice that for the first game, your parent referenced the game as a challenge. Before the second game, your parent referenced it as a threat.

In psychology, these are referred to as a "gain" (i.e., a challenge) and a "loss-prevention" (i.e., a threat). Understanding the difference between a challenge and a threat can be a huge factor in your success. Viewing a competition as a challenge means you can gain from it by winning, and there is nothing to lose. Viewing the competition as a threat means you have *everything* to lose. Go back and reread the first section of this chapter and see if you can now point out the differences between what was said before your first and second games.

As an example, in the 2019 Champions League semifinals, Barcelona took a commanding lead in the two-game competition by winning the first game at their home field, Camp Nou, by a score of 3-0. Liverpool would need to score four goals without conceding any goals in the second game at Liverpool's stadium, Anfield, to go to the Champions League final. To make things more difficult, two of the three starting forwards, Salah and Firmino, were out of the game with injuries.

Barcelona was threatened because they had everything to lose. It would be a huge challenge for Liverpool to score 4 goals against one of the greatest clubs of all-time, but the two backups did not see it that way. They realized they were expected to lose and loved the challenge. Sure enough, Divock Origi and Georginio Wijnaldum each scored two goals to lead their team to the 4-0 victory they needed to advance to the Champions League final. It was unbelievable and largely because these two men took it as a challenge to beat the seemingly unbeatable odds, even though they were two unknown backups.

Given how surprising this was, many people could not believe this happened nor would happen again. However, the next night in the other Champions League semifinal match, Ajax was leading the Tottenham Hotspurs 2-0 at halftime and 3-0 overall because of their 1-0 win in the first game at their home stadium, Johan Cruijff Arena. Forward Lucas Moura of the Tottenham Hotspurs realized they needed 3 goals to advance to the finals (due to away goals) and had only 45 minutes to do it, while needing to avoid conceding more goals to Ajax.

Ajax team members were threatened at this point because they had everything to lose in the second half. Sure enough, Lucas Moura realized his side had nothing to lose and scored three second half goals to lift his side to their first Champions League final ever. Two of the most unbelievable Champions League semifinal games of all-time were played on back-to-back nights and highlighted the difference in viewing a soccer game as a challenge versus viewing the opposition as a threat. Now, let us consider a few ways to ensure you are being challenged and not threatened:

1. The first thing to consider takes no effort on your part. The scoring in soccer is already additive, meaning that each time your team scores, you are rewarded with a goal on the scoreboard. Many students have trouble with school because of the subtractive nature of homework assignments. Specifically, many students believe they start an assignment or test with a 100%, and each wrong answer takes away points. **Counting**

upwards instead will not eliminate stress about performance, but it will place students in a "gain" mindset rather than a "loss-prevention" mindset.

2. Anson Dorrance, the coach of the University of North Carolina Women's Soccer Team, has won 22 national titles and achieved the ranking of Sixth-Best Sports Dynasty of All-Time by Beckett Entertainment. When Dorrance's team went up by a point or two, they refused to shift their attitude towards defense. They did not want to protect a lead (i.e., cultivate a "threat" attitude). Instead, they wanted to score more (i.e., maintain a "challenge" attitude). By attacking a challenge, you will develop the skills needed to remain in this frame of mind. **Therefore, it is important to understand that you should never let up on an opponent.**

This concept may offend some people, but during seasons and tournaments when goal differentials can determine who wins the championship, it is important to always keep the "challenge" attitude and keep scoring. For example, consider the United States Women's National Team in the 2019 World Cup. In their first match, they played Thailand. At halftime, they had a convincing 3-0 lead, which would have been more than enough, considering Thailand was a low-ranked opponent, and the U.S. team was ranked #1 in the world. However, did the U.S. team coast for the rest of the game? Nope, they scored 10 more goals in the second half to win by a final score of 13-0. Again, letting up is not the mindset you want to have.

3. **Ask yourself before a match which mindset you are currently in.** You do not need to tell anyone else that you are doing it. Simply ask yourself, "Do I have a 'challenge' mindset right now, or a 'threat' mindset?" It is often difficult for you to realize in a match which way you are thinking if you have not been trained to do so. When you make sure you are in a 'challenge' mindset, you will win many more games during your career.

4. **Avoid using guilt or threats to motivate yourself to perform better.** While threats may help provide short-term results, the long-term costs of the emotional damage may be too much for you to overcome. Using fear as a motivator takes the fun out of playing soccer. A "threat" conveys the message that you do not believe you can do it, whereas a "challenge" says that you believe you *can* do it. Therefore, do not say things to yourself like, "I will not be able to play with my friends", or "I will be in a bad mood for the rest of the day." Also, avoid statements of guilt like, "My family spent a lot of time and money for me to be here; I cannot let them down." If thoughts like those enter your mind, dismiss them. Instead, tell yourself this is a challenge you will overcome.

Understanding the difference between the challenged and threatened attitudes can make it easier to perform. Remember that each practice and game is a challenge, so avoid using guilt to motivate yourself. Though it may work in the short-term, it often results in stagnant growth in the long-term. Lastly, do not expect yourself to be perfect all at once. **It takes time and many games for the lessons and techniques described in this book to impact your soccer game positively.** If this chapter seems familiar, there is a similar chapter in the book, *Soccer Parenting*. Therefore, if you are a soccer parent reading this book, order a copy of the *Understand Soccer* series book, *Soccer Parenting,* to learn many things, including how to give feedback effectively to your child, how to work with the coach to ensure success for your child, and the top 10 things every soccer player needs to hear from their parent.

Since viewing the game as a challenge instead of a threat is one way to help reduce anxiety before a game, let us discuss a few other ways to reduce it. Some symptoms of performance anxiety include:

1. Racing heart rate
2. Rapid breathing
3. Dry mouth
4. Tight throat
5. Trembling hands, knees, and voice
6. Sweaty hands

7. Cold hands
8. Nausea
9. An uneasy feeling of butterflies in your stomach
10. Restlessness

Some ways to overcome anxiety before a match are:

1. **Recognize that pre-game jitters are normal.** Accept the nervous energy you feel and reframe it as excitement rather than nerves. This topic is discussed in great detail in the *Understand Soccer* series book, *Soccer Tryouts,* as most people feel more nervousness before a tryout than before an important game. Avoid misinterpreting the excitement you feel before the game as fear. The adrenaline rush you experience is your body's way of getting you ready for game time. Understand its importance but avoid focusing on it. Once the match starts, the feeling will go away after a few minutes, and you will instead become focused on what you must do in the game.

2. **Prepare both mentally and physically.** Arrive at the game with plenty of time, so you are not rushed. Ensure you do a complete warm-up involving dynamic stretching so that your body is physically ready to perform. Worry and confidence are at opposite ends of the spectrum. When confidence is strong, it tends to push worry out of the mind, so control what you can before the game to ensure confidence *during* the game.

3. **Visualize your performance.** Mentally rehearsing the likely game scenarios that you will come across will reduce your level of anxiety when you find yourself in those situations.

4. **Consider deep breathing.** This can be done alongside visualization and needs to be practiced to become effective. Taking full breaths through your nose while expanding your stomach (not your chest or upper back) will help release tension from your body and mind.

5. **Distract yourself.** Distracting yourself prior to the game could involve doing homework, listening to music, joking around with teammates, reading a book, watching motivational videos on YouTube, looking at memes, or browsing inspirational pictures. All these activities can prevent your mind from generating negative thoughts about the game. Memes are one way I distract myself, if needed. If memes are something you enjoy too, be sure to follow me on Instagram **@UnderstandSoccer** for fun soccer facts, as well as a ton of soccer memes!

YouTube: If you would like to learn about challenges versus threats in a video format, then watch the *Understand Soccer* YouTube video: How to Have More Fun Playing Soccer.

Chapter 3

Locus of Control

For the context of this book, the "locus of control" is a term used in modern psychology to show how much a person believes they can control the outcomes of events in their lives. **Specifically, a soccer player with an external locus of control believes that external circumstances like the weather, teammates' opinions, and what past coaches have taught are what shapes their future. Whereas a soccer player with an internal locus of control believes their own work ethic, perseverance, mindset, attitude, and feelings are ultimately what determine their future.**

An external locus of control places the blame on circumstances you cannot control. It will leave you feeling like there is nothing you can do to make your current situation better and that "it is what it is." **Whereas, the internal locus of control mindset allows you to learn from your present situation, work to improve what you already have, and overcome obstacles that are placed in front of you.**

In the chapter on the fixed mindset versus the growth mindset, we pointed out Freddy Adu. Freddy Adu had an external locus of control, which is very often paired with the fixed mindset. By seeing his skills as being gifted to him (i.e., given to him by outside forces), he had an external locus of control and believed that it will happen if it is meant to be.

A player who embodies the opposite of this is Lionel Messi, the forward for Barcelona and Argentina, who is one of the greatest players of all-time. He has an internal locus of control knowing that his abilities were developed over time. Granted, many people view him as gifted and Cristiano Ronaldo, a winger for Manchester United/Real Madrid/Juventus and Portugal, as having to work for everything. However, if you look at their backgrounds, they come from very similar situations and have very similar attitudes of wanting to be the one in control. Throughout their careers, they wanted to determine the outcome of games for their team. In fact, the following quote by Lionel Messi reveals that he worked hard to become a success. He stated, "It took me 17 years and 114 days to become an overnight success." This quote reveals that he knows there is no such thing as an overnight success. He believes in controlling his circumstances and working hard to be the best he can be. **Similarly, he constantly strives to beat his previous self and become even better with each passing year.**

One of the many tricks Messi uses is to control more things leading up to the game. **Many players have very long routines the day before games and the day of games to**

increase their control over their process and ensure they can perform at their peak come game time. Although Messi's routine is extensive, let us break down his meal preparation, according to *Men's Health Magazine*.

A week before a match, Messi decreases his carbohydrate intake and increases the amount of protein and water he consumes. Also, Lionel Messi eats vegetable soup with spices at the beginning of meals. Some spices Messi uses are chili powder, coriander, ginger, and turmeric. Chili powder helps prevent inflammation, increases blood flow, and burns fat. Coriander helps prevent inflammation, fights infection, and boosts memory. Ginger helps prevent inflammation, reduces pain, improves digestion, and increases cardiovascular health. Turmeric helps prevent inflammation, delays aging, aids digestion, and reduces pain.

Without as many carbohydrates, Messi may experience slightly less energy in the days leading up to a game. Cutting carbohydrates forces his body to become more efficient with the sugar levels in his blood. Once Messi reintroduces the carbohydrates a day before the game and the day of the game, it increases his energy because of the carb loading. Messi's ideal dinner the day before a game has meat (e.g., fish, chicken, or prawns), green veggies, an orange, and potatoes. Six hours before match time, Messi eats porridge and egg whites. Then,

90 minutes before the game starts, Messi eats fruit. Now, do you need to go to this extent by starting a week before each game to see results? Probably not but understanding that the more you increase your locus of control and the more you feel your control will increase your confidence and performance on the field.

If you are interested in learning more about proper soccer nutrition to ensure you have the energy to perform amazingly in every single game, then consider grabbing the *Understand Soccer* series book, *Soccer Nutrition*. This book breaks down the meal plans of soccer's greats, reveals the keys to pre-game and post-game nutrition, and discusses the few things that make the biggest impact if you are wanting the most out of your meal plan for your time and money.

In conclusion, remember that taking responsibility for everything you can take responsibility for may be slightly overwhelming at first. **However, it will be a relief in the long run, because if you are responsible for it, then that means you can change it.** The most tiring and emotionally exhausting things are those you cannot control. By increasing your locus of control, you will decrease the things that drain your mental and physical energy.

Activity: Locus of Control

For each of the following statements, pick the option you most agree with to see where you sit on the locus of control spectrum. The answers are in the appendix at the end of the book.

A. It is too hard to be good at soccer these days.
B. I know it is up to me to become good at soccer.

A. Joining a good soccer team depends on being in the right place at the right time and knowing the right people.
B. Becoming a success in soccer is a matter of hard work; luck has little or nothing to do with it.

A. What happens to me in soccer is my own doing.
B. Sometimes, I feel that I do not have enough control over the direction my soccer career is taking.

A. In the long run, people receive the respect they deserve in soccer.
B. Unfortunately, an individual's worth in soccer often passes unrecognized, no matter how hard they try.

A. The coach is the major factor in how well I play for a team.
B. I have the greatest control over how I play for a team.

A. Without the right breaks, one cannot be an effective coach of a soccer team.

B. Capable people who fail to become good coaches have not yet taken advantage of their opportunities.

A. Players who cannot get along with other players do not understand how to get along with others.

B. No matter how hard you try; some teammates will not like you.

A. When I make plans in soccer, I am almost always certain that they will work.

B. It is not always wise to plan too far ahead in soccer because many things turn out to be a matter of luck anyway.

Chapter 4

Identity Capital

Identity capital is our collection of mental assets. These are the skills, thought processes, mindsets, and resourcefulness we assemble over time. Additionally, it is how we solve problems, how well we can speak to others, and, to an extent, even how we look. Ideally, these are developed over the course of your entire life and are built moment-by-moment with each new experience. However, most people still have not developed these abilities after their traditional schooling has finished.

Traditional schooling is meant to lay the groundwork and provide the basics for having a fulfilling life. **After your traditional schooling is completed, it is up to you to keep building on the framework set in place by your years in elementary, middle, and high school.** Granted, some people attend college or a university, but this basically provides specific knowledge in your major, without providing many of the real-world skills that everyday people need to succeed on their own terms.

To be completely honest, I lacked identity capital as a child. I was very self-conscious and unconfident. In soccer games, the only time I performed well was when I believed I was the best player on the soccer team. If there were other children who were better than me, I would shut down in fear and not play to my abilities because I thought they were better and should lead the team.

To make matters worse, I had tons of excuses for anything that did not go my way. There was always something or someone else for me to blame. After years of listening to a soccer mentor on how to play well and reading many books to improve my communication abilities, increase my confidence, and decrease my fear of failure, I can now enjoy soccer and contribute to the team even if I am not the best player on the team. I take on challenges that scare me but will ultimately help me grow and build my identity capital.

People who go through an identity crisis often will say things like, "I need to find myself." Whereas, people who focus less on a crisis in their own head and focus on building up their identity capital will say things like, "I need to create myself." Yes, this implies you will need to work to create yourself. Excitingly, you will be building yourself in a way you have chosen which ensures it will feel less like work and more like play.

When I first started writing soccer books, it felt like work because there was so much to learn and a lot of things to do. However, after I built identity capital as an author, writing seemed less like work. Now, writing is my way of helping soccer players improve their confidence and individual skills, and this is what I have consciously chosen to build my identity capital around. It is something I enjoy doing daily and even though parts of it can be exhausting, it is very rewarding to see my skills as an author grow as I help soccer players like you in ways I really needed help with when I was your age.

In terms of soccer, never building up the identity capital by playing on teams slightly outside your comfort zone, being the person to demonstrate drills with your coach while not worrying if you make a mistake, and never working towards your desired position on the soccer field can lead to having to confront some harsh truths. You will notice an increase in your sadness, you will probably question if you like soccer, and will have a nagging thought in the back of your mind telling you to quit playing soccer because you are not good enough. Taking the steps to avoid these unproductive thoughts is how you build your identity capital.

Therefore, when selecting a team to join or a position to play in soccer, pick the one that will provide the most identity capital. Pick the team where you will build the best relationships, learn a lot of techniques, and grow the most. Pick the position you can see yourself playing for many years to come and the one that seems the most fun to you. **Do not worry if you have all the skills necessary right this moment. Just make sure you do not give up learning and growing to ensure you will become great at the position you want on your team of choice.**

Avoid picking a team that is the most prestigious if it means you will sit on the bench the whole season. Being a benchwarmer means you will not be obtaining much in-game experience. However, you do not want to join a team where you are clearly the best because then you will probably practice/play with sub-par competition and will not grow like you would if you played against soccer players who are slightly better than you.

Here are 10 ways for you to boost your soccer identity capital immediately:

1. Build more experience on the field by playing with older kids and better kids, while not being afraid to make mistakes;
2. Identify the goals you want to achieve in the next month, season, year, and five years;
3. Ask your coach for more responsibility on your team;
4. Read soccer books to gain knowledge;

5. Avoid comparing yourself to others; instead, only compare yourself to your previous self;

6. Make it a habit to practice for at least 30 minutes per day, six days per week;

7. Analyze the play style of the soccer players you admire to learn from them;

8. Watch interviews of the soccer players you admire to better understand their mindset;

9. Befriend your coach to increase your communication skills and time on the field; and

10. Do what you fear most in soccer.

In conclusion, there is not just one thing you must do to ensure you will have all the identity capital you will ever need. Playing time and quality training are needed to improve and build your skills. **Once your abilities are built, they are very easy to maintain and are easier to build even further.** Similar to when you first started playing soccer, the beginning is the toughest part because you have so much to learn and so many skills to develop. However, as you begin to add skills and abilities, it becomes easier and fun to add more!

Chapter 5

The Comfort Zone Trap

Many soccer players, coaches, and parents fall into the trap of the comfort zone. I am not perfect either and I fall into the comfort zone trap on occasion, too. However, it is important to understand what it means to stay there. Learning the importance of traveling outside your comfort zone will make it increasingly easier for you to grow. Therefore, let us start by looking at the different zones you will travel through as you go from your comfort zone to your growth zone.

As you can see in the image, your goal is to go from the comfort zone through the fear and learning zones to arrive at the growth zone. Sure, the comfort zone feels safe because you feel in control of your surroundings and the things you are working on. **However, the comfort zone is not ideal because when you are comfortable, your learning slows or stops altogether.** Taking a step outside your comfort zone puts you in the fear zone, which is also known as the "terror barrier."

In the fear zone, you realize that you will need to learn skills to arrive at the growth zone. The fear zone is often where someone lets other peoples' opinions affect their thoughts. Most people will attempt something new to step out of their comfort zone. The problem is that they do not realize they are the most vulnerable and have the lowest self-confidence immediately outside of their comfort zone. **Sadly, most people will create excuses and reasons that whatever they are attempting to do is too difficult and they will go back to their comfort zone feeling upset and defeated.**

Excitingly, as the person reading this, you now understand that you can go back to your comfort zone after stepping into the fear zone, but the trick is to learn more. **You have low self-esteem in the fear zone because you do not yet know enough about what you are attempting to do.** However, learning what to do, whether that be from your own mistakes or by someone else's mistakes, will allow you to enter the learning zone.

In the learning zone, you will pick up the skills and abilities needed to overcome your problems and challenges. **For soccer players, you can learn from reading, a coach/parent, watching soccer, watching "how to" videos about soccer on YouTube, and from attempting something yourself to figure out how to improve.** The learning zone requires you to put in work, but it is the last step before achieving your goal in the growth zone.

Finally, after having learned and implemented what you needed, you arrive in the growth zone. The growth zone is an exciting place to be because it is where your dreams in soccer become reality. It allows you to be okay with making mistakes because you know you will contribute to your team's success every single game. In this zone, you will experience some level of anxiety, but you can turn it into motivation and fuel for productivity. **By learning to overcome your fears, you will feel great. You will love playing soccer, and your enjoyment of it will keep growing.**

Now that you understand how to travel to the growth zone (also known as your "stretch zone"), you can begin to expand the things you are comfortable doing because your growth zone will eventually turn into your comfort zone. Sadly, you must not go too fast, or you risk going past the growth zone and into what is known as the "panic zone", a term coined by Andy Molinsky, an author, researcher, and the Professor of Organizational Behavior at Brandeis University's International Business School.

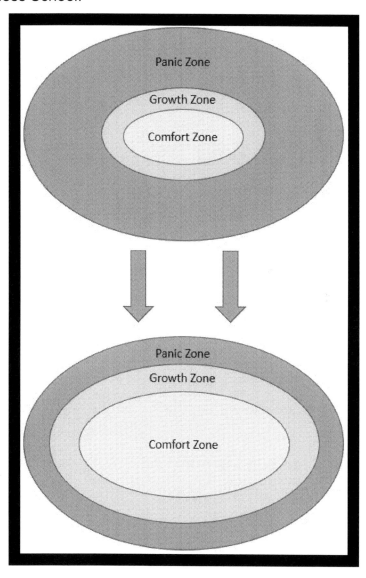

As you can see in the image, the panic zone (also known as the snap zone) is where you will end up if you are taking on too much and not allowing enough time to recover from the anxiety and stress often associated with growing. Therefore, the threshold of anxiety overtakes your capacity to handle the stress. You can often see the panic zone with your teammates or even in yourself because you all work so hard to be better but mentally burn out and often obtain physical injuries. **As you grow in your comfort zone, the potential things that can sap your energy and cause you stress decreases.**

An example of moving to the growth zone is when you realize you want to beat a defender 1v1 as the defender is backpedaling towards their net. You attempt to dribble past them, get stopped, and now become fearful that you will never be able to dribble past the defender. Then, you remember that you must improve your knowledge and skills to overcome that fear and understand what it takes. As you learn new abilities, you practice them on defenders. For the first several tries, you still cannot beat a defender 1v1. Still, you keep your head held high because you realize you can learn a ton from your mistakes. **You mentally go over what went wrong, change it, and finally learn to beat a defender 1v1 almost every time.** This is great because you have entered the growth zone.

At this point, you are excited to see that moving from your comfort zone to your growth zone is a learnable process. Now that you have arrived at the growth zone, you say to yourself, "Instead of just learning one skill and focusing on using it right now, I am going to focus on five of them at once." You attempt to learn the shot fake, the self-pass, the step over, shooting a driven shot with precise form, and passing correctly using the inside of your foot. You attempt to learn what you need for each one at the same time and realize you are not spending enough time on any of them individually. You burn out and distance yourself from learning these new skills. Sadly, you find yourself not as excited about soccer as you were when you were learning just one thing thoroughly. **Learning five things at once and not going very in-depth in one thing is how you enter the panic zone and stunt your growth.**

It is important that when you enter the growth zone, you avoid the panic zone. You must avoid depleting all your emotional capital by doing too many things at once without the recovery and rest/sleep needed for a soccer player to succeed. If you are interested in a great night's sleep every single night to help your body and mind recover, then grab the *Understand Soccer* series book, *Soccer Sleep*. Once you master a skill, then move on to the next one.

In conclusion, the growth zone eventually turns into the comfort zone because as you grow and learn new things, they become increasingly comfortable for you. **If you are thinking to yourself, "It seems like it is a lot of work to become better," then consider that to be a good thing.** If it were easy, everyone would do it! Therefore, since there is some hard work ahead of you, you will quickly become better than your opponents and even the other players on your team! If you do not do this, you can still enjoy soccer, but you will lose out on the continual growth that someone else on your team will gain.

You can further your growth by reading books in the *Understand Soccer* series, practicing the skills you read about, learning from your mistakes, and becoming a continual learner of this beautiful game. It is great to know that, as you go on the journey of continued improvement, you will realize that things seem to become easier. However, it is not that things are becoming easier; it is just that *you are becoming better.*

Chapter 6

Compounding Skills

In finance, there are two terms that describe how your bank savings account could grow in value: (1) compound interest; and (2) simple interest. These are fancy terms for an easy concept. "Simple interest" is how most people think of the effort they give in soccer. Let us say you are just starting your soccer career and have not yet worked to improve your soccer skills at all. In this case, you are starting with zero strengths. (If you play FIFA, you can also think of strengths as the "talent points" that you use to upgrade your attributes.) If you are starting at zero strengths, then you must deliberately practice, which means you must learn and work hard to gain five strengths from practice. Therefore, "simple interest" means every time you train and enhance your skills, you obtain exactly five more strengths. Therefore, if you train seven times, you gain 5+5+5+5+5+5+5 strengths (or 35 total strengths). The following image shows the simple interest of your strengths:

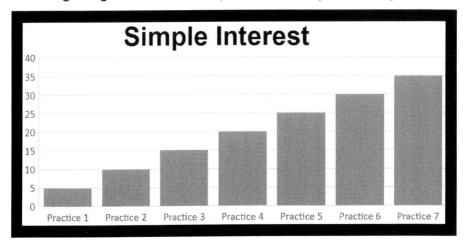

How soccer (and your bank savings account) actually work is through compound interest. Consider that you are starting at zero strengths, and you practice seven times. However, because strengths compound, you gain five strengths from the first practice. You can now invest all those extra strengths into your next practice. Instead of gaining another five strengths (as shown in the simple interest concept), you gain six strengths from your second practice. Now, you are at 11 strengths, and you can use them in your next practice, from which you will gain eight strengths. After your third practice, you are now up to 19 strengths.

Your strengths keep compounding with each additional practice, so you gain 10 strengths in your fourth practice, 13 strengths in your fifth practice, 16 strengths in your sixth practice, and 20 strengths in your seventh practice.

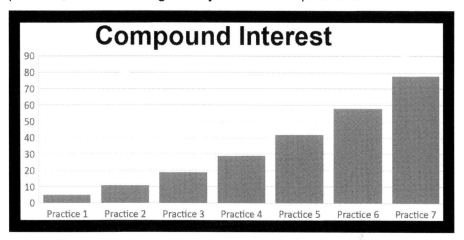

Remember that from simple interest, you gained five strengths each practice and went from zero strengths to 35 strengths after seven practices. However, compound interest shows us that we gained a total of 78 strengths (5+6+8+10+13+16+20) from the seven deliberate practices. This is more than double the 35 strengths gained from the simple interest example. **Therefore, by obtaining soccer skills and proper techniques, and then deliberately practicing them, you will grow your strengths quicker than most people realize.**

Think about how it is much easier to learn a bicycle (overhead) kick for a soccer player who can shoot well, correctly time a ball in the air, and has good jumping abilities than it is for a new soccer player who cannot do any of those things yet. **Therefore, your skills and abilities compound on top of each other.**

A similar term related to soccer is "never miss a cone." Too many trainees do not realize that missing one cone each lap for a four-lap drill is four cones missed. Add those missed cones up over the course of the training session, and they equate to roughly 40 missed cones. Add that up over an 8-week course, and that is 320 cones missed. Add that up over an entire career, and the soccer player who skips cones is missing up to 30,000 or so opportunities to become better. Remember that you are already spending time training, so you might as well make the most of it. Missing one additional rep each lap does not seem like much in the moment, but it surely prevents you from compounding the skills that will make you better more quickly.

Also, remember that when you do not practice, you lose your strengths. **You are either becoming better or becoming worse; there is no such thing as keeping your strengths exactly the same.** For every 3-4 days that you rest and do not learn or develop your soccer skills, you can expect to lose strengths. After not practicing for a long weekend, you will often notice that you cannot run for as long without becoming tired, and your foot skills are slightly worse than they were only a few days ago.

Some ways to gain strengths are:

1. Read or listen to books on how to become better at soccer;
2. Learn from your coach(es) or parent(s);
3. Learn from a teammate's advice after you made a mistake;
4. Learn from your own mistakes at practice and in games;
5. Watch the world's best soccer players on television; and
6. Watch "how-to" soccer videos on YouTube, such as on the *Understand Soccer* channel.

Compounding your skills, speed, strength, knowledge, confidence, etc. is very important. **Learning about more things and implementing them will create a huge change in you.** After all, bad players take little seriously. Average players take games seriously. Good players take practice and games seriously. Great players take learning, nutrition, sleep, warm-ups, independent work, weight training, conditioning, flexibility, practice, and games seriously.

Above all, remember that some things are more important than others, and there is not enough time to do everything. If the concept of compound interest excites you, check out Jeff Olson's book, *The Slight Edge*. This is a life-changing book. It teaches how, by doing small things—ones that are easy to do but also easy *not* to do—you can forever change your future and have a life full of success.

Chapter 7

Setting S.M.A.R.T Goals Using Step Ladders

The Merriam-Webster Dictionary defines a goal as "the end towards which effort is directed." Determining the goals that you want to achieve as a soccer player will go a long way to help you become a much better soccer player than your teammates and/or opponents who do not set goals. **Generally, all goals you set for yourself should be written down and S.M.A.R.T.**

S.M.A.R.T. stands for:

S = Specific (who what where)
M = Measurable (weigh)
A = Attainable (which)
R = Relevant (why)
T = Timely (when)

S.M.A.R.T. Goal #1: Specific

Your goal must be **specific**. Otherwise, you will not focus your efforts to achieve it. When determining whether your goal is specific, you should answer the following three questions:

1. **What do I want to accomplish?** You must first decide what you want to be your goal. For example, learning how to shoot a driven shot for the first time.

2. **Who is involved?** Ideally, you will have a mentor providing the steps for you. You will need to be involved, too, since you want to learn how to shoot a driven shot.

3. **Where must I go to achieve it?** You must figure out where the goal needs to be met. For a soccer player learning a driven shot, this would be on a soccer field, in your backyard, or on a street without cars.

S.M.A.R.T. Goal #2: Measurable

Your goal must be **measurable**. If you cannot measure it, then it will be hard to determine whether you are becoming better or if you have achieved the goal. Therefore, you must weigh your goal. Weighing something is a method of measurement. A soccer player learning how to shoot a driven shot can measure each step of the process by how many goals they can score in practices and games. Also, you can measure it by the increased power and accuracy in practices.

S.M.A.R.T. Goal #3: Attainable

Your goal must be **attainable**. Learning how to shoot a driven shot is very attainable. However, having a goal to score

100 goals in a single game is not. Make sure you set your sights on something that can be achieved or is slightly past what you think you can achieve. This requires that you ask yourself how you can attain it. For example, learning the steps and spending several practices using deliberate practice to learn how to shoot a driven shot will allow you to score more goals in seemingly no time.

S.M.A.R.T. Goal #4: Relevant

Your goal must be **relevant**. To determine whether your goal is relevant, ask yourself why this goal is important to you. If your aim is to become a better soccer player, then learning how to shoot a driven shot is very relevant, as it will increase the number of goals you score in a season.

S.M.A.R.T. Goal #5: Timely

Your goal must be **timely**. Being able to shoot a driven shot is great but learning it when you are 50-years old and have stopped playing or coaching soccer 20 years ago is not a timely goal. Also, expecting to spend one hour to learn how to shoot with the speed and accuracy of Cristiano Ronaldo is also not timely because that is an unrealistic timeline.

To determine the timeliness of your goal, you must first determine when you need to achieve it. Giving yourself a reasonable deadline will ensure you do not have much time to slack off or too little time to realistically accomplish the goal. A reasonable deadline will ensure you have enough time to accomplish the goal without losing focus.

The Step Ladder Method for Success

Now that you understand S.M.A.R.T. goals, the best way to bring your goals into fruition is to use the "step ladder" method. **Using the step ladder method, a large goal like consistently and powerfully shooting a driven shot can be broken down into parts that are much more manageable.** This is because when using step ladders, the only way to travel to the next step is if you have already taken the one before it.

In the image, you must start at the base of the ladder and master Step One. Then, you can move on to Step Two, and so

6. Ensure Your Hips Are Pointing Where You Want The Ball To Go
5. Make Sure You Bring Your Back Leg Forward
4. Follow Through And Land On Your Shooting Foot
3. Have Your Toe Down And Out While Your Knee Is Facing The Target
2. Plant A Foot Away When The Ball Is Stopped
1. Approach The Ball Diagonally

forth. **However, most soccer players rarely realize that each one of these steps is a building block that you need to lay down to travel to the next step.** If we take the image and look at it from the side instead of from the front, this becomes clearer that it looks more like a staircase:

					6. Ensure Your Hips Are Pointing Where You Want The Ball To Go
				5. Make Sure You Bring Your Back Leg Forward	5. Make Sure You Bring Your Back Leg Forward
			4. Follow Through And Land On Your Shooting Foot	4. Follow Through And Land On Your Shooting Foot	4. Follow Through And Land On Your Shooting Foot
		3. Have Your Toe Down And Out While Your Knee Is Facing The Target	3. Have Your Toe Down And Out While Your Knee Is Facing The Target	3. Have Your Toe Down And Out While Your Knee Is Facing The Target	3. Have Your Toe Down And Out While Your Knee Is Facing The Target
	2. Plant A Foot Away When The Ball Is Stopped	2. Plant A Foot Away When The Ball Is Stopped	2. Plant A Foot Away When The Ball Is Stopped	2. Plant A Foot Away When The Ball Is Stopped	2. Plant A Foot Away When The Ball Is Stopped
1. Approach The Ball Diagonally	1. Approach The Ball Diagonally	1. Approach The Ball Diagonally	1. Approach The Ball Diagonally	1. Approach The Ball Diagonally	1. Approach The Ball Diagonally

As you can see, each step is built upon the previous one. Often, players will only focus on the certain steps they want to learn and avoid spending time on the other steps. However, the previous image shows that each step should only be taken after the previous one has already been mastered. Also, when setting goals, not having actionable steps makes the goal of shooting a driven shot correctly a huge goal. **When you can break it down into its parts, each step seems more manageable and easier to do than if they were all lumped together.**

In the book written by Gary Keller and Jay Papasan, *The One Thing*, this type of goal setting is also referred to as "goal setting to the NOW." **Set a future goal, then drill down to what you should do right now.** If your goal will take roughly one year to accomplish, then figure out what you need to have done six months from now, one month from now, one week from now, by the end of the day, and what you can start right now. In conclusion, using S.M.A.R.T. goals will help you determine exactly which goals you should set for yourself and how to plan the steps to make the goal much easier to achieve.

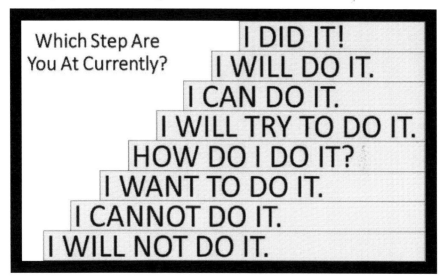

To learn how to score and when to use many of the different types of shots, like the driven shot, grab the *Understand Soccer* series book, *Soccer Shooting & Finishing*.

YouTube: If you would like to learn how to set S.M.A.R.T. soccer goals in a video format, then watch the *Understand Soccer* YouTube video: How to Set S.M.A.R.T. Goals.

Chapter 8

Deliberate Practice

Deliberate > Purposeful > Habitual Practice

If you have read the *Understand Soccer* series books, *Soccer Coaching* or *Soccer Parenting,* then this chapter will look similar to the chapter on deliberate practice in those books. However, this book is for the soccer player who is working on the field, so this chapter will describe the soccer player's role to ensure they practice deliberately.

As a soccer player, it is important that you do not just practice to "get touches." There are certain hotspots around the world that produce outstanding performers, like country singers from Tennessee, hockey players from Canada, and soccer players from Brazil. These hotbeds for talent have training programs that involve deliberate practice.

Deliberate practice is systematic. Regular/habitual practice often means dribbling, shooting, and passing in ways you have done before and are comfortable performing. **Deliberate practice requires attention and is accompanied by the specific goal of improving your performance using**

your knowledge of where the practice needs to go and how to travel there step-by-step.

For a soccer player, this is where having a soccer trainer is important. **An experienced soccer trainer will give you the training you need, which will allow you to develop very quickly and deliberately.** However, make sure the soccer trainer is teaching the specifics on how to do things. If you are just dribbling through cones, passing, shooting, and it appears you are just "getting touches" without really learning how to do everything with proper form, then this is likely a trainer to stay away from. Expect measurable progress in a reasonable period of time for yourself. Think about it: by having an in-person or online soccer trainer, they will invest the time and their 20 or so years of knowledge and skill to teach you how to more quickly succeed. Your abilities will skyrocket much quicker than the opponents in your league and even your teammates.

Habitual/regular practice (e.g., trying to juggle) is not as good as purposeful practice (e.g., a player setting a goal for each practice, such as juggling the ball 30 times in a row). Purposeful practice is not as productive as deep and deliberate practice. **Again, deliberate practice is purposeful practice, but it includes the information and knowledge needed to understand how to find your weak areas and improve them.** The goal is to advance quickly by progressively focusing on the areas just outside your comfort zone. For example, juggling with the tops of your feet towards your toes 30 times in a row to better settle the ball out of the air.

When you first start playing soccer, everything is new and just going through the reps will be a new experience in which considerable learning will occur. **But if you train on the same things that you are already good at doing, with no meaningful plan to progress, then you will likely overlook small errors and miss opportunities to improve.**

Mindless activity is the enemy of deliberate practice. The danger of practicing the same thing again and again without focusing on making small improvements is that you believe you are becoming better because you are working on your soccer abilities. In reality, you are likely reinforcing habits that have room for improvement and wasting practice time by merely reinforcing those imperfect habits. The natural tendency of the brain is to turn repeated actions into habits. **Deliberate practice breaks the overall process down into parts, allows you to identify your weaknesses, work on different ways to improve those areas, and then brings all the training together to improve quickly.**

As a soccer trainer, one of the biggest areas my trainees struggle with, especially at a young age, is

shooting a driven shot with correct form. At a high level, a trainee must start diagonal to the ball, then plant a foot away from the ball. Next, on the foot the player is striking the ball with, they must have their toe down and out with their knee facing the target, so they can use the bone of their foot. Afterwards, they must follow through, land on their shooting foot, bring their back leg forward, and point their hips where they want to score. This is a lot for anyone to learn if this is the first time they are working through the steps.

Therefore, instead of working on all the steps at once, I have found it is best to start the trainee planted about a foot away from the ball and focus on striking the ball with the bone of their foot. After 10-15 repetitions of becoming comfortable striking with the bone, I will have them take a step to work on correctly planting next to the ball and continuing to strike with the bone of their foot. Then, after another 10-15 repetitions, I will have them work on following through to land past the ball. **The process is to add in one additional step each time until they are comfortable with that level and then adding another step until they are comfortable shooting driven shots with the correct form.**

You may be wondering how Brazil has so many well-developed soccer players. Well, the most popular form of soccer in Brazil is referred to as *"futebol de salão."* This is 5v5 soccer and is oftentimes played on a basketball court. During each game, each player has 6X more touches than they would in the same time span of an 11v11 soccer game. The Professor of Soccer at the University of São Paulo, Emilio Miranda, says it is Brazil's "laboratory of improvisation." **Adding many more touches with little room and/or little time to make decisions forces players to improve their recognition of patterns and learn how to act in many soccer situations.**

As a soccer player, it is important to understand the concept of deliberate practice so that you can advance your skills quickly and productively, now that you have the soccer knowledge to do so. Recognizing that this is one of the best ways to teach someone a task with many steps will also make it easier for you to determine if a coach is good for you.

If you are interested in learning more about deliberate practice, consider picking up the book *Talent is Overrated* by Geoff Colvin, in which Colvin describes how Benjamin Franklin used deliberate practice to improve his writing skills, and Mozart used deliberate practice to become one of the greatest musicians of all-time at a young age. He confirms the old saying: *"It takes about 10 years and about 10,000 hours of deliberate practice to become an overnight sensation."*

Chapter 9

The 80/20 Rule

The 80/20 principle was first observed by the Italian economist Vilfredo Pareto. As a result, the 80/20 rule is also known as the "Pareto Principle." He first observed it while looking into land ownership in his home country of Italy. His first work on the principle stated that 80% of the land was owned by only 20% of the population. He then looked at many other fields and noticed that the same principle applied. Therefore, the 80/20 rule states that 80% of the results are due to only 20% of the things you do. **In soccer, roughly 20% of your habits have 80% of the impact on your performance.**

Despite this truth, so many players equally weigh everything, both in their minds and in their practices. This is because many soccer players have their priorities in practice backwards. Often, players care more about the cool foot skills and a powerful shot than being able to make a perfect 10-yard pass to the correct foot, lead your teammate making a run, or receive a pass with one touch that perfectly sets you up to take a shot. I will be completely honest when I say I fell into this trap in my early high school soccer years, as well. The things I practiced the most were my shot with the ball stopped, tons of foot skills without being able to use any of them in a real game situation, making sure I had terrific nutrition, and I weight trained 5-6 days per week. Sadly, because I could not effectively receive a pass near the net or dribble past an opposing player, I hardly ever had the opportunity to take a shot.

Let us consider a former teammate of mine, Joey Tinnion, who was a forward for a Division 1 university soccer team, played for the professional team Waza Flo Pro, and is now the coach of a college soccer team. Joey was an all-state forward who scored nearly 30 goals in his junior season of high school. During halftime at one of our high school matches, he told me he practiced the same few skills over and over again, and they seemed to always work. I should have been more intelligent and realized that what he said was outstanding advice. **If a player only ever uses four foot skills, then you can bet they will become fantastic and very effective with those four skills.**

I was unwise at the time, so I thought his advice was bad because I believed that you should know a ton of skills to be great. I ignored his advice for the next couple of years. I continued practicing jab steps, single scissors, double scissors, self-passes, rolls, six different shot fakes, three-directionals, step overs, elasticos, rainbows, etc. I was a "jack of all trades and master of none." Sadly, if you do not master any skills, the skills you attempt in a game will not often work when you use them. **This leads to a ton of frustration for a soccer player who is practicing a ton of hours but is not spending those hours working on the best things.** With his four skills, Joey Tinnion kept scoring. On the other hand, me with my 12+ skills, found it hard to even shoot until I realized that I needed only a few skills to become someone who averaged two goals per game.

Next, let us discuss scoring in soccer. There are many ways to score in soccer, but only a few of the ways will provide the most goals throughout your playing career. **In the following image, notice that 80% of a soccer player's goals on average will come from either the driven shot or the bent shot.** Only 20% of the goals that a soccer player scores on average will come from pass shots, headers, trivelas, toe pokes, bicycle kicks, heel shots, or goals from other body parts. Therefore, most of your time should be spent on perfecting the driven shot and the bent shot.

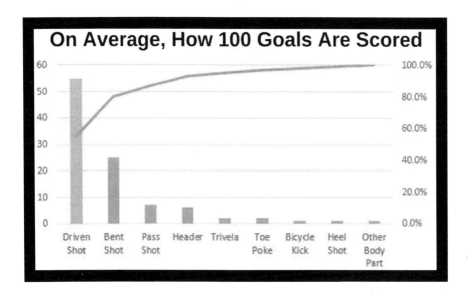

On Average, How 100 Goals Are Scored

In conclusion, the 80/20 rule states that 80% of your results come from 20% of your actions. Therefore, to become better a lot quicker, you must focus on the few things that will make the biggest impact within the shortest time. Some of these high-impact areas are:

-Passing the ball 10+ yards without error;

-Knowing exactly how to use an attacking touch;

-Learning the Big 3 foot skills;

-Learning how to take a driven shot; and

-Knowing where to push the opposing player while defending.

Working on these few things will help you 10X your game much more quickly than less important things, like being able to juggle the ball 100 times in a row, having a 500-lb deadlift, or stretching for 30 minutes before and after each game.

Additional Reading

If you are curious about the Big 3 foot skills that every soccer player should master for the three main situations you will be in when covered by a defender, then grab the *Understand Soccer* series book, *Soccer Dribbling & Foot Skills*. **This book will teach you how using only three foot skills will make it so you will have plenty of games where you are taking at least 10 shots per game, which almost guarantees you can consistently score two goals per game.** Without knowing what those three skills are or without being able to perform them, you will be like the player I used to be, who lacked the confidence needed on the soccer field.

Additionally, although *Soccer Passing and Receiving* is a terrific guide for players to learn exactly how to pass with correct form and receive the ball to score easily, it is the least-purchased book in the *Understand Soccer* series. Remember that passing and receiving are at the foundation of the "Individual Soccer Player's Pyramid" mentioned in the preface of this book. **If you have read other books in the *Understand Soccer* series but not *Soccer Passing and Receiving*, then you are not following the 80/20 principle.** Instead, you are working on the flashy aspects of soccer without focusing on the major area that will improve your game the quickest.

Passing and receiving are at the base of the "Individual Soccer Player's Pyramid" because it is the foundation that all soccer players need to build an outstanding soccer career. Therefore, I highly suggested you read that book next before going on to any of the other technical books within the "Individual Soccer Player's Pyramid."

YouTube: If you would like to see a video to learn about the 80/20 rule, then watch the *Understand Soccer* YouTube video: How to Practice Less and Score More.

Chapter 10

Shooting with Your Opposite Foot

Notice that the title of this chapter says to shoot with your "opposite foot" and not your "weak foot." **By referring to your opposite foot as your weak foot, you are displaying a limiting belief.** If you treat your opposite foot like a weak foot, then you will likely not take the necessary steps to develop it. You will probably avoid practicing with it and avoid developing it to become comfortable using it in a game. How you perceive things in both soccer and in life generally dictates how you will execute and become better. This concept is known as "reframing" and is used by modern psychologists to help people find the silver lining in situations by using constructive words and statements to help people achieve their goals in life.

Most people agree that your beliefs help shape the words you use, but few people realize the opposite is true, too. The words you use help shape your beliefs, which is why you often hear from others that you should "watch what you say." If you are not careful, you might end up believing something that holds you back.

The form for shooting with your opposite foot is the exact same form as shooting with your dominant foot. **Understand**

that you do not need to take a free kick just as good with either foot or that you should be able to shoot from 30 yards out just as easily and accurately with your opposite foot. Being able to shoot with your opposite foot means that if you are inside the 18-yard box, you should be comfortable going to your right foot or to the left foot, whichever foot is going make it easier for you to take a shot. A good defender will attempt to push you to your opposite foot. The opposing defender will give you a bit more space to push the ball, accelerate, and shoot with your opposite foot if you are willing to use it.

Any time I am playing defense, and I am going up against an attacker who only uses one of his feet to shoot the ball, I am very pleased. They are usually easy to shut down, and it takes less effort to prevent them from shooting because you know in which direction they will attempt to go. **All you need to do is give them space towards their opposite foot.** You know they are unlikely to utilize their opposite foot. Even if they do use it, they will not be comfortable enough to take an effective shot. This is why you should make it easy to succeed on the field by developing both of your feet.

Although there are players who have had successful soccer careers using only one foot, such as Mesut Özil, these players are the exception and not the rule. Personally, I did not learn to use my opposite foot until I was 14 years old. As a child and early teenager, I had a lot of limiting beliefs. **One of those limiting beliefs was "I am not naturally gifted at using my opposite foot, so this must mean I should not use it."** Keep in mind that it never registered to me that I was good with my dominant foot only because I used it exclusively for the first 10 years of playing soccer!

Finally, I swallowed my pride and realized that I needed to change. I needed to use my opposite foot. However, I was so ashamed of my form that I was unwilling to use it in a practice or a game.

When I came to this conclusion, it was during a summer when a World Cup was held, as they occur only every four years. I was inspired by the soccer players in those games, and I was still young enough that I had minimal responsibilities outside of soccer. Therefore, every day over the course of that World Cup, I would watch the games and practice shooting for 30 minutes to an hour a day, 4 to 5 times a week with my opposite foot. I would go to the side of my parents' house and work on shooting with my opposite foot. I would either work on shooting for distance/power by striking the ball between my parents' house and my next-door neighbor's house or take shots off the wall of my parents' brick house to work on accuracy. (Note: ask your parents for permission before shooting soccer balls at your home).

For me, it started off very rough. I could not kick the ball with the bone of my foot more than 15-yards and my form was horrible. It felt awkward and I can guarantee you that it looked awkward too. However, I made up my mind that I would keep practicing until I could use my opposite foot. **Notice what was said in the previous sentence. It stated, "I will keep doing it until."** I learned this mindset later in life from the mentor Jim Rohn, who reframed my view on how to approach a task, project, or situation I wanted to attain a certain outcome. Luckily, I intuitively understood it at a young age.

Your mindset is critical because generally, anytime you set out to do something, it will take longer and be more difficult than you originally planned. There are times where a plan you put in place does not work and then you decide to give up. As a result, you still will not be able to use your opposite foot very well because you lacked the mindset and the consistency to keep practicing until you could do what you had initially set your mind to do. Some tips when it comes to shooting with the bone of your opposite foot are:

1. **Make sure you are very angled to the ball (i.e., 45° at the absolute minimum but ideally 60° to 75°).** This is so you can start becoming comfortable with pointing your toe down and out while using the bone of your opposite foot to strike the ball.

2. **Make sure to bend your leg at the hip *and* the knee.** Too many of my trainees only bend at the hip which prevents their strongest muscle, their quadriceps, from being used to increase the power of their shot.

3. **Practice, practice, practice.** Make sure you do enough repetitions so that you will start to develop a consistent form. Clearly, you will want this form to be perfect from the beginning, but if you are uncomfortable shooting with your opposite foot and have not really practiced using it yet, then your first goal is to become more comfortable using your opposite foot to strike the ball. Even if you are worried about your form needing correction, first focus on making it consistent.

A professional player who has a great story about using his opposite foot is David Villa. David Villa had played for Barcelona, Atlético Madrid, and the Spanish National Team but was almost unable to because of an injury he sustained when he was four years old. Villa, who was a right-footed player, suffered a broken right leg. With the guidance of his father to push him to use his left leg, he was able to come back stronger than other players his age because he started off so young being able to use both feet to dribble, pass, and shoot. His ability to use both feet laid the groundwork for a fantastic career as a striker in soccer.

Keep in mind that improvement takes time. If you do not do it correctly right away—or even over the course of a few weeks—then that is okay! Know that it took me about two-and-a-half months to even become comfortable enough to use my opposite foot in practice—and I was *still* uncomfortable even *attempting* an opposite-footed shot in a game! Therefore, if you feel uncomfortable using your opposite foot, then practice using it in your free time, either outside your house, on a soccer field, or on an open piece of land to work on developing an opposite foot that you can rely on to score.

If you want to learn more about the exact techniques needed to strike the many types of shots in soccer or if you are interested in step-by-step instructions on how to score by using most of the ways described in the previous chapter's chart, then grab the *Understand Soccer* series book, *Soccer Shooting & Finishing,* to increase the power of your shot by up to 100% and become more accurate. These will allow you to feel great after games, knowing the team relied on you to win.

Chapter 11

Warm Up Your Mind

It is important for a soccer player to warm up their body before a game. However, most soccer players forget that they should also warm up their minds. You can have a fully warmed-up body, but if your mind is not prepared to play, then you will find your performance lacking. **Therefore, consider the following keys to a great pre-game mind warm-up:**

1. Have a Routine
2. Focus on Process Behaviors
3. Mentally Rehearse

Key #1: Have a Routine

Having a pre-game routine ensures that you have a consistent plan to help you before a game and to increase your internal locus of control. Pre-game routines consist of drills and dynamic stretches that push blood into the muscles and synovial fluids into the joints. To learn how to warm up your body before any game, as all soccer players should, grab a copy of the *Understand Soccer* series book, *Soccer Fitness,* to learn the exact steps needed to increase your performance and avoid injury. Also, your pre-game routine should focus on the mental side of your game too. A routine is like a funnel that channels your focus to ensure you are ready to play soccer. Pre-game routines help you remain focused on the important items while avoiding mental distractions. **For example, you can have a few phrases to tell yourself before every game, such as:**

-I am calm, cool, and collected.

-I am a goal-scorer.

-I am a hard worker.

-I am prepared for this moment.

-I am focused.

-I am unstoppable.

-I am relentless.

-I am unshakable.

-I am a leader.

-I am a winner.

Key #2: Focus on Process Behaviors

Next, remember that soccer is a team sport with 22 players in total and referees who also help to decide the outcome of the game. Therefore, be focused on what you can control. **"Process behaviors" represent what a soccer player has control over and can perform regardless of how the game is unfolding. Things like being aggressive, playing**

hard, staying level-headed, keeping your head up, having fun, communicating, and being positive with yourself and teammates are examples of "process behaviors." A soccer player can stay committed to these attitudes throughout a game, whether or not it is going well. Focus on the process and you will increase the likelihood of positive results happening.

Key #3: Mental Rehearsal

Think about the things you can do in the game to make sure you perform most effectively. Given that I play as a striker for my team, some things I mentally rehearse and visualize before games are:

✓ Keeping my head down to keep my form together while shooting;
✓ Swiveling my head so that I know where the opposition is when I receive a pass from a defender or midfielder; and
✓ Using the self-pass when a defender reaches for the ball.

Mental Routine + Physical Routine = Success

In conclusion, soccer is as much a mental game as it is a physical one. Focus on both your mental and your physical routines prior to game time to ensure your mind and body are ready to go. Understand that process behaviors are things you can always control because they help describe your mindset. **Additionally, mentally rehearse the items which you know will make the biggest impact on your game.** These rehearsals are position-specific and should differ for each player. Finally, remember that you can also have a morning routine upon waking to start off your day right and ensure your eventual success.

YouTube: If you would like to learn how to warm up your mind before a game in a video format, then watch the *Understand Soccer* YouTube video: Soccer Warm Up - How to Get Your Mind Ready.

Chapter 12

Mentally Tough

In the chapter on locus of control, it explained that you must take responsibility for everything you can control. **However, there are certain things outside your control that you just must accept and move on, such as the weather, the field you play on, and the officiating.** According to a former United States Marine, Michael Eldridge, "It is mind over matter; if you do not mind, then it does not matter." Therefore, as a soccer player, you must strive to be mentally tough.

At Next Level Training, the premier soccer training program in Michigan, there is a saying in large letters on the wall that says, "It is 75°F and sunny." Many soccer players make the excuse that it was raining, windy, too hot, too cold, muddy, etc. My soccer mentor, Aaron Byrd, jokingly says to players making weather excuses that even though it was raining for your team, it was 75°F and sunny for the other team. He is poking fun at the trainee's attitude because the opposing team had to play through the same poor conditions as the trainee's team did. **However, because the opposing team did not concern themselves with things they could not control, they were better able to prepare for**

the things they could. They had a tougher mindset to avoid having the weather and field conditions as excuses for why things were not going their way. Remember, winners WIN! Having bad weather or poor field conditions as an excuse reveals a weak mindset. However, a team should understand the pros and cons of each condition to help their team's game

Different Field Types			
	Attacking	**Defending**	**Goalkeeping**
Dry Turf Field	Helps	Hurts	Even
Wet Grass or Turf Field	Hurts	Helps	Hurts
Indoor Field	Helps	Hurts	Even
Short Grass Field	Helps	Hurts	Even
Long Grass Field	Hurts	Helps	Helps
Boarded Field	Helps	Hurts	Hurts
Muddy Field	Hurts	Helps	Helps
Uneven/Clumpy Field	Hurts	Helps	Hurts

plan. See the chart below:

Even if you disagree with one or two of the above examples, you still must understand that poorer field conditions generally help defenders because passing and foot skills become more difficult to use. The better the field conditions, the easier it is for attackers to score and use their strengths. For goalkeepers, conditions around the net are their only concerns. **Use these conditions to your advantage when possible.** Make sure you increase the number of shots you take when playing in the rain or on a wet field because the goalie will have a much tougher time judging and handling the ball. It is best to know that being a defender on a muddy, uneven, clumpy, or long-grass field will make it easier for the other team's attackers to make mistakes and thus for you to stop them. Understand that being an attacking player on a perfectly trimmed grass or turf field will make it much easier to dribble and pass.

A great way to reframe unfavorable situations that are out of your control is to find the silver lining. First, finding the silver lining teaches your mind to look for the good in every situation and to be more grateful, which is so important. Second, you can benefit from the silver lining. Try it! **Say aloud, "[insert the thing you dislike here] benefits me because [insert the silver lining here]."**

For example, say you are a defender and are playing in a game when it is 100°F outside. You can complain all you want, but it will not change the temperature of the game. To find the silver lining, you might say, "It is 100°F outside, and that benefits me because forwards and strikers on the other team must play in this heat, too, and all their explosive cuts and runs will be more tiring than usual. The heat gives me an advantage in the game." Being able to reframe situations that seem bad into situations that are good will help you become a mentally tough soccer player.

Chapter 13

Do Not Worry About a Bad Call

In soccer, as in most other sports, referees ensure fairness for both teams. Sometimes, the referee may make decisions and award calls that you believe are unfair and undeserved. However, by constantly blaming the referee and implying that their actions are the only reason for your loss, you are telling your subconscious mind to blame others for the poor outcomes in your life. Surely, referees make terrible calls sometimes, and I am not suggesting that there are never times when they make mistakes. **However, 99 times out of 100, once a referee makes a call, they will stay firm in their decision.**

As a player complaining, you are wasting your time, sapping your energy, and reducing your emotional capital on something that cannot be changed. **Even worse, this bad call is distracting you from the rest of the game and the steps needed to overcome the referee's bad call.** Make sure you are focusing on the things that can be changed. Even if the referee made a terrible decision at the end of a game that cost your team a goal and ultimately the victory, remind yourself there were 89 other minutes of soccer played where you had many other opportunities to score to ensure that it was not in the referees' hands to change the outcome of the game. Let me restate that a good soccer team will aim to win by a few goals, so even if the ref makes a terrible call or two, your team still has room for error on the referees' part.

The reverse of being a calm player who respects the referee is yelling at the referee any time they make a mistake. Having refereed games myself, I know I am less likely to make a call in favor of that team if they are constantly hassling me and judging every single decision I make. Therefore, make sure the coach has selected a captain or someone on the team who is designated to talk to the referee. Should the referee make a mistake, the coach can have the designated person calmly explain that they disagree with the referee's call, explain why quickly, and then move on mentally from there. **Even if that player provides valid arguments, the referee likely will not change their decision but may look to make up for that decision later in a game or at least make sure not to make a similar error again.** Soccer players find it embarrassing when their teammates yell at the officials or lose their composure because it hardly ever helps the team. Worst of all, your teammates may look down on you for often complaining and being easily distracted by the referee's actions.

In conclusion, harassing a referee generally only make things worse. If you want to be a great soccer player, you will need to lead by example. By pointing out the referee's flawed calls, you are reinforcing the idea that others need to change for you to receive what you want. Also, yelling at the referee will make the referee less likely to make a call in favor of your team later in the game. Although referees can make mistakes (and often do), remember that they are just humans trying to do their best, just like you. Give them a break or two, show them respect, and focus on the areas of soccer you can control.

YouTube: If you would like to learn how to not worry about a bad call by watching a video, then watch the *Understand Soccer* YouTube video: How to Not Worry About A Bad Call.

Chapter 14

Cristiano Ronaldo's Mindset

What good would a soccer book on mindset be without discussing the mindset of one of the greatest soccer players ever to play the game? From his goal-scoring prowess to his huge cabinet of trophies, Cristiano Ronaldo (also known as "CR7", due to his uniform number) is an outstanding performer whom the world is lucky to have witnessed play.

His unique outlook in soccer is defined as follows:

-He is a continual learner;

-He has confidence in his actions—even if he comes across setbacks;

-He works harder than his competitors; and

-He has the desire to win.

He is a Continual Learner

Cristiano Ronaldo has said, *"I feel an endless need to learn, to improve, to evolve, not only to please the coach and the fans but also feel satisfied with myself."* This quote of Ronaldo highlights that he realizes continually learning is the best way to get ahead and necessary to stay ahead. Since he was a young soccer player, he has been focused on daily improvement. To reach his ever-larger goals, he must take the deliberate steps to achieve his short-term goals that ultimately add up to creating his long-term successes at the pinnacle of soccer. Most players work hard to travel to the top. Ronaldo worked incredibly hard to be there and continues to put in the work to stay there. At Cristiano Ronaldo's level, he realizes that developing his skills both on and off the field is necessary to grow continually as a soccer player.

He Has Confidence Despite Setbacks

Cristiano Ronaldo understands that confidence is a learnable skill, and it can be developed with practice. He has even said, *"In my mind, I'm always the best. I do not care what people think, what they say. In my mind, not just this year but always, I'm always the best."* These are powerful statements that some may view as skewed, boastful, or even harmful. However, Ronaldo understands that he needs to have confidence in what he does—even if other people think he is too over the top with his remarks and beliefs.

Ronaldo viewed himself as the best long before he ever was considered one of the best. There can be little doubt that his self-belief has helped make him a top performer. Because Ronaldo truly believes that he is meant to be the best, he trains hard to become more knowledgeable than his competition. There are countless setbacks we can point to on the field but often it is the off-the-field problems that are the most difficult challenges. At 15 years-old, Ronaldo was diagnosed with a racing heart according to his mother, Dolores Aveiro— something most athletes could not overcome. He decided soccer was too important and had the operation to fix the problem so he could come back to the game he loves. This example reveals that he does not let setbacks stop him, even though they may slow him down in the short-term.

He Works Harder Than His Competitors

Though some natural talent has made it possible for him to be decent at soccer, he became great because of his work ethic. After all, it is easy to find players who have talent who never become the player who so many parents and coaches expected them to become. **Cristiano Ronaldo has a first to arrive and last to leave training mentality with practice to ensure no one is receiving more from training than him.** In fact, he trains 3 to 4 hours per day to remain at peak physical state and to ensure that his skills are game ready.

Let us look at how he works hard to prepare for a game and the ways he ensures quick recovery after a game. **The night before a game, Ronaldo is a huge advocate of obtaining enough sleep.** He knows that great sleep is critical to recover from training and to be rested for the training the following day. Do you want to learn more about how to obtain a great night sleep every night and feel well-rested in the morning to have the energy to tackle all the tasks you usually feel to sluggish to do? Then, pick up a copy of the *Understand Soccer* series book, *Soccer Sleep*, for the step-by-step guide to obtain terrific sleep every night, so you will feel well-rested in the morning and happy to take on the day. In fact, Ronaldo aims for at least eight hours of sleep a night.

Upon waking, Ronaldo likes to do a short workout in the morning to ensure he can fit in exercise wherever he can. In an interview with *Goal.com*, Ronaldo revealed that he even performs abdominal workouts to start his day and before going to bed. According to Ronaldo, *"If you get into a routine, then it makes it easier. It will become a habit."* Similarly, nutrition is no light matter to Ronaldo. He prefers up to six small meals each day because *"a good workout must be combined with a good diet."* Like Lionel Messi, Ronaldo eats meals high in protein, with whole grains, fruit, and vegetables.

Before a match, Ronaldo has pre-game habits. He starts his warm-up even before his teammates start. Part of this involves looking at his own reflection to psych himself up mentally for the game. **Like Alex Morgan, Ronaldo understands the importance of staying as relaxed as possible.** His thoughts will be on what will happen in the game while moving, stretching, listening to music, and having fun to lighten the serious mood of playing in soccer matches with millions of eyes watching him.

After the game is completed and often won, he has post-game habits that help ensure his health and long-term success. Ronaldo goes so far to say, **"Recovery is more important to me than actual training sessions."** Well, when you play at least 50 games a year, it is understandable why Ronaldo takes his recovery so seriously. From drinking water and consuming food to refuel his body to varying between hot and cold baths, he goes to great lengths to promote the recovery of his body. He even goes for post-game swims. Remember, most soccer player will stretch for a few minutes and likely grab some food as their only post-game habits. All of Ronaldo's productive habits led Juventus' medical staff to say that he has the physical capacity of a 20-year-old when he joined the club at age 33.

He Has the Desire to Win

Former Manchester United teammate Quinton Fortune leaves us with this final thought on Cristiano Ronaldo's mindset: *"He had the desire to win, and his talent was unbelievable. You get a lot of talented players who don't have the desire to do the work, but Ronaldo puts in the work. His desire got him to where he is today. I've never seen anything like it because every single day he came into training, he was doing extra: shooting, dribbling, scissors, going to the gym, wanting to be stronger, and quicker to be better every single day."* Interested in learning about all the potential positions in soccer, including CR7's position as a winger? Then, grab the *Understand Soccer* series book, *Soccer Positions*.

YouTube: If you would like to learn about Cristiano Ronaldo's Mindset in a video format, then watch the *Understand Soccer* YouTube video: Cristiano Ronaldo's Mindset.

Chapter 15

Visualization

Renato Susnja, former Division 1 college midfielder and now an outstanding soccer trainer at Next Level Training in the metropolitan Detroit area often says that it is important to ***"anticipate, do not react."*** This attitude allows you to imagine what will happen *before* it happens. Expecting a play to happen, which is a type of in-game visualization, affords you the time needed to make an action plan.

Visualization before you take a shot is nearly as effective as actually having taken a practice shot according to the famous Australian psychologist, Alan Richardson, who conducted a sports experiment proving visualization's worth for athletes. This is huge because you know how you are always better going through a drill the second time than you are the first time in practice? Well, having your first lap in your mind will make the second lap way better, which is really only the first lap in reality. Grab a copy of the *Understand Soccer* series book, *Soccer Passing & Receiving*, to learn more about how to make a plan and how it will increase the number of goals and assists you will earn in a season.

Let us look at Alex Morgan, the forward on the Women's United States National Team, who is an Olympic gold medalist and World Cup Champion. Alex Morgan has stated, "I never get too hyped up too early before a game — I feel like that leads to having restless legs and mind." Alex Morgan says she prefers to **"Do a lot of mental visualization and use breathing techniques to calm myself down before a game."** Therefore, she likes to use pre-game visualization to ensure she can go over likely situations in the game, even before the game starts. This allows her to determine what she would do to score, provide an assist for a teammate, take a penalty kick, or act in a particular situation.

It is as easy as sitting in a chair, on the field, or even in the car for five to ten minutes before a game while breathing deliberately. Harvard Medical School says to take deep breaths. The air coming in through your nose should move downward into your lower belly and let your abdomen expand fully. Avoid breathing where your chest is going up and down as this can lead you to being more anxious. Now, breathe out through your mouth or your nose, if that feels more natural. **Avoid shallow breathing because it feels tense and constricted, while deep breathing produces relaxation.** Next, visualize the likely scenarios you will encounter in a game. Scenarios have been broken down by position:

Forwards:

-Perfectly placing a penalty kick;

-Easily using a body feint (i.e., jab step) in a 1v1 against a defender;

-Shooting on net while keeping your head down; and

-The great feeling of scoring or earning an assist.

Midfielders:

-Making the perfect pass to a forward who scores;

-Using the self-pass to beat players on the opposing team who are reaching in for the ball;

-Working past the point where your body is tired and wants to slow down; and

-Scoring from outside the 18-yard box with a powerful shot.

Defenders:

-Blocking the opposing team's shots while keeping your hands behind your body;

-Flawlessly executing the stepover when you have the ball and your back is facing the net you need to score in;

-Stopping an opposing forward who is attempting to dribble past you; and

-Clearing the ball to the perfect spot for your forwards to take possession.

Goalkeepers:

-Reacting correctly to stop an opponent's penalty kick;

-Throwing/kicking the ball accurately up the field to a teammate;

-Working hard to save the other team's shots; and

-Yelling directions to your defenders when you want them to adjust their positioning.

In conclusion, using visualization will help you achieve the 10,000 hours of deliberate practice to achieve mastery in soccer. Also, visualization will make the game easier because you have already experienced it once before in your own mind. Just 5-10 minutes of visualization can produce huge results for you and your team. Thankfully, you do not need to be perfect to start; you can begin by using the guidelines above, and in time, you may find even better ways to visualize your own success.

YouTube: If you would like to learn how to get better at soccer without even touching a ball, then watch the *Understand Soccer* YouTube video: Playing Soccer Using Visualization.

Chapter 16

Future Truths

Like pre-game and in-game visualization, you can use future truths to help yourself advance quickly up the soccer rankings. **Specifically, future truths are a way of training your mind to become comfortable with something you want to happen in the future.** Yes, this technically is a current lie. But are you willing to lie to yourself today (in a very positive way) to produce the future you truly desire?

Personally, I am willing to do that! Here is a shortened version of the future truths I told myself long before they ever came true:

-I have an outgoing personality;
-I am at peace;
-I am funny;
-I am a #1 best-selling soccer author;
-I have thick skin;
-I am a great storyteller;
-I am secure;
-I am a source of inspiration;
-I take feedback well; and
-I am fulfilled.

If you keep telling yourself a future truth, then you will associate that truth with the person you want to become. More importantly, you will figure out the actions you need to take to make those future truths become a reality. For example, let us say you are a girl who wants to be a forward for the United States Women's National Team. One of the easiest things to do to achieve this goal is to tell yourself you will be a forward on the United States Women's National Team. Say it out loud! "I will be a forward on the United States Women's National Team." Say it out loud one more time! Now, let me ask you two questions:

1. Was the future truth you stated uncomfortable to say?
2. Did you feel like you were lying to yourself?

Remember, it is a current lie, but it is not a future lie. It is a future truth. **Are you willing to lie to yourself in the current moment to become the best player in your league or would you rather be true to your current self and probably not even be the best player on your team?** That is a decision for you to make but the more you say future truths, the more you will believe them. If you say a statement like, "I am an average soccer player," it is a self-fulfilling prophecy, so you will not take the time and energy to learn how to be the best player in your league. However, if you say future truths repeatedly and take the action required to achieve it, you will make the future truths come true. Have future truths that will make it easier for you to make decisions like, "Should I go watch television this afternoon or would working on my shot with my opposite foot for 30 minutes be more helpful for me to become a forward on the United States Women's National Team?"

You do not need to know every step you should take from this point until you achieve your future truth. You just need to start, work hard, never give up, and understand you will better see the next steps needed as you begin down the path towards your future truth. Even if you do not have your driver's license yet, just imagine you want to drive somewhere. Would you wait to leave until all the lights are green or would you just drive and understand that you will have some red lights on your journey you must overcome but will have a clearer view of the path as you travel down it? Here are some future truths you can implement into your mindset today, sorted by position:

Everyone:
-I am continually learning;
-I am a leader;
-I communicate well;
-I am not afraid to make mistakes; and
-I am open to feedback.

Forwards:
-I score easily;
-I am fast;
-My foot skills allow me to take many shots;
-My shots are accurate; and
-I have powerful headers.

Midfielders:

-I create opportunities for my teammates to score;
-I am calm in the middle of the field;
-I am a playmaker;
-I am great at shooting outside of the 18-yard box; and
-I have amazing endurance.

Defenders:

-I am a terrific shot-blocker;
-I am physical;
-I easily steal the ball from the other team;
-I am great at winning the ball in the air; and
-I am dominant in 1v1s.

Goalkeepers:

-I tell my defenders what to do;
-I make tons of saves;
-I have a short memory of goals I let in;
-I start my team's counterattacks with accurate throws and kicks; and
-I am tough.

Coaches:

-My players love playing for me;
-I provide feedback in ways that my players are receptive;
-I learn from my mistakes;
-I am a winner; and
-I enjoy working with parents.

The above list of future truths is not all-encompassing, but it provides a good starting point for a soccer player based on their position, as well as the first list of future truths that applies to everyone. Even though this book is specifically for soccer players, you can use the concept of future truths in every area of your life. Use it for your schoolwork, friends, family, spiritual beliefs, etc. Do not forget to add your personalized current truths, as well. **Act like the person you want to be in order to become them.** As the wise philosopher Socrates once said, *"Be as you wish to seem."*

If you are interested in a more complete list of "I am" statements and future truths that you can use to build your confidence and mindset, then make sure to get the free "Morning Habit Checklist" at UnderstandSoccer.com/free-printout.

Chapter 17

It is Okay to Make Mistakes

Steve Corder, a former Division 1 college coach and soccer player at the University of Detroit Mercy, once said something to a group he was training that left a lasting impression upon me. Steve stated, ***"In soccer and in life, you will make hundreds of thousands of mistakes over your lifetime. Once the mistake occurs, it no longer matters that you made the mistake; it only matters how you react to the mistake."***

Most people see mistakes and failures as the same thing. **However, failures are mistakes that have been left uncorrected.** If you make a mistake, learn from it, and then correct your actions—this is how you can quickly succeed. Life's greatest lessons are usually learned at the worst times and from the greatest mistakes. In the quote in the previous paragraph, Steve teaches that you cannot get caught up in your past actions. Instead, you must do whatever you can in the present to place yourself in the best situation to succeed in the future. Therefore, if you just made a mistake, the best thing you can do is to take responsibility for it, figure out what happened, learn from it, and then move on.

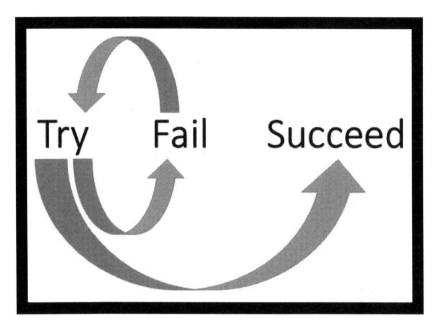

When recovering from a mistake, do not make the mistake worse by worrying about it. Recover from it as quickly as you can to avoid wasting time in the present that can be better used for the future. Personally, I suffered for years from the fear of not being perfect. This caused me not to do many things because I was worried about what others would think. Even worse, I was crippled with fear because of my laser-like focus on the mistakes I made. When I did something, I had to check it three times. Then, after reading several books to improve my view of mistakes, I swung too far in the other direction to where I was not concerned *enough* about errors, to the point at which I was not even checking my work at all. This was bad because I mentally became okay with making mistakes, but I was not taking the steps necessary to *learn* from them.

When working on something, check your work once. Any more than that and you are likely just wasting time—unless you are performing something very serious and it is the difference between life or death. Not checking your work at all will create sloppy/lazy mistakes. Again, mistakes are great learning tools, but there is a fine line between doing your best in a reasonable period of time but still making a mistake as opposed to being lazy/sloppy and making *careless* mistakes.

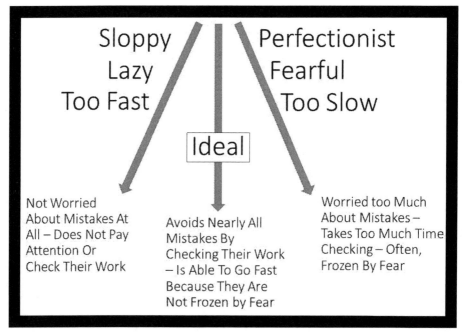

For example, perhaps your coach is demonstrating a dribbling and foot skills drill that your team will be practicing. Perfectionists would have anxiety about going through the drill because they might make mistakes. Perfectionists would want to be the last one in the line to see others perform the drill before starting and so hopefully no one will see if they make a mistake. On the other hand, sloppy players will go through the drill and make mistakes at seemingly every cone because they did not pay attention as the coach was giving directions. **It is ideal to be the person in the front of the line who is helping the coach demonstrate the drill, is actively watching and listening to the coach's directions on what to do at each set of cones, and understands he or she may make a mistake or two on their first lap or when helping to show how to perform the drill.** However, this same person will have done a good portion of the drill correctly and will have learned from his or her mistakes when going through the drill the second time. If you are looking for drills with specific coaching points to use in practices in order to increase your player's skills, grab the *Understand Soccer* series book, *Soccer Drills*.

In conclusion, avoid lazy mistakes, but do not be so worried that you must be perfect in everything you do. After all, **perfectionism is an excuse for procrastination.** Oppositely, Albert Einstein was right when he said, *"Anyone who has never made a mistake has never tried anything new."*

YouTube: If you would like to see a video on why it is okay to make mistakes, then watch the *Understand Soccer* YouTube video: Are Mistakes Bad or Good for You?

Chapter 18

Reducing the 10,000-Hour Rule

When learning anything in life, there is a learning curve involved. **A learning curve describes how much time is needed to become better at something.** In this chapter, we will further explain its impact and how to reduce your learning curve. K. Anders Ericsson, the author of the book, *Peak*, points out that to become an expert in the field of your choosing, it takes about 10,000 hours of deliberate practice. Some fields require less, and others require more, but 10,000 hours is an easy number to remember. Your learning curve dictates your journey to the 10,000-hour mark.

Everyone's learning curve is slightly different, as is the learning curve for each skill you want to learn. Though not every player can become Lionel Messi or Cristiano Ronaldo, they can still become world-class with enough deliberate practice, learning, and hard work. Playing soccer well involves an increasing return learning curve, as shown in the following image:

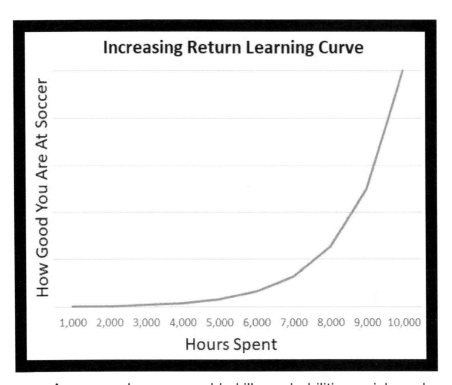

A soccer player can add skills and abilities quicker when they have a solid foundation. For a soccer player just starting out, there is a ton to learn, and their feet are not as coordinated yet. Often, soccer players start at a young age, so their minds cannot grasp things as quickly yet, and they do not have much strength in their undeveloped bodies. **However, as a soccer player matures both mentally and physically, it becomes much easier to understand how to learn skills and when to use those skills in games, such as when to pass and how to receive passes with the correct form, how to strike a soccer ball five different ways, how to understand in-depth game planning to take advantage of an opposing team's tactics, etc.** Therefore, the increasing return learning curve means that a soccer player is acquiring skills, speed, and strength at an ever-increasing rate, until the maximum learning potential is reached. Soccer falls under this category because of the complexity of the sport, and all the variables that can be learned.

On the other hand, the diminishing return learning curve shows a higher increase in skill at the beginning. However, it decreases with time, until it reaches zero additional skill for each additional hour spent. At this point, the person has achieved the maximum skill level. **The diminishing return learning curve indicates that, initially, there are huge gains in learning with little time invested.** This typically occurs with skills that are less complex.

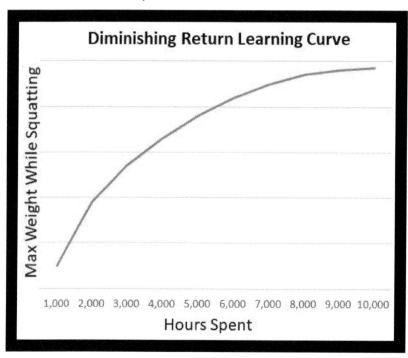

Consider the example of the diminishing return learning curve in the previous image. For a person attempting to increase their weight for a barbell back squat, they realize huge increases in strength very early. However, as the person's knowledge on form, nutrition, and training increases, the additional weight a person can add is very small with each new workout.

Weightlifters find it easy to work towards squatting 250 lbs. It takes planning and a lot of time to increase their squat to 500 lbs. Most weightlifters will spend their whole careers working to have a 750 lb. squat, and the few individuals with favorable genetics, large femurs, and big body frames will find they generally max out at around 1,000 lbs. The reduction in pounds is a terrific example of diminishing returns for less complex tasks.

At this point, you are likely comfortable with how learning curves work but may be thinking, "Wow, 10,000 hours is a lot to spend playing soccer to become better at it!" I definitely agree. 10,000 hours of deliberate practice is no small feat and going down the path of becoming a great soccer player takes time and dedication. **However, there are a few loopholes that will allow you to attain 10,000 hours in significantly less time.** Because there are many ways to reduce the 10,000-hour rule, let us apply the logic we learned in the chapter on the 80/20

Principle to figure out which ones will provide us the largest impact with the least amount of work.

The loophole that will provide you with 80% of the results in 20% of the time is finding a mentor. A mentor does not need to be Lionel Messi or Cristiano Ronaldo, as these individuals likely would not have the time and would be very expensive. Furthermore, they are so incredibly skilled that most soccer players working with these two superstars would give up before realizing their full potential because in their minds they would not believe they could ever be like Lionel Messi or Cristiano Ronaldo.

It is best to start with a mentor who is a few years ahead of you and can teach you the things you need to become better at performing to quickly become a much more effective soccer player. As you grow, you can add different mentors who have new and/or advanced skills. An in-person mentor would be the most ideal, but because this can cost a significant of money and tons of time, most people find that mentoring through books and online videos is better for them.

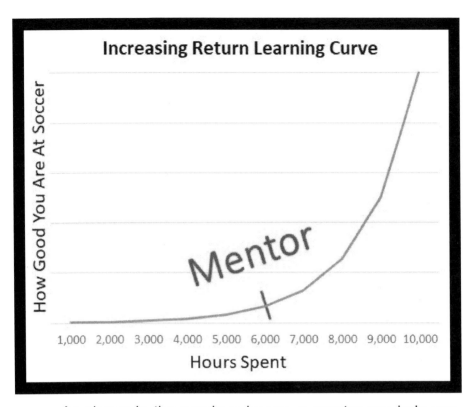

As shown in the previous image, a mentor can help you jump the learning curve. **By finding and learning from a mentor, you can invest the time they have spent playing, learning, and making mistakes into your own skills and abilities so that it may take you only 4,000 hours of deliberate practice guided by a mentor to reach the same point as a soccer player who spent 10,000 hours without a mentor.** There is a Russian expression stating, *"A dumb person makes the same mistake over and over again. A smart person learns from their mistakes. A wise person learns from someone else's mistakes."* Therefore, I challenge you to be the wise person who learns from other people's mistakes.

A mentor can give you a guide and/or model to follow that will help you figure out the path quicker than if you attempted to figure it yourself. A $10 "how-to book" on soccer, or a $47 video course on soccer, are both very cheap when you consider that you will be taking someone else's years of successes, failures, studies, and experiences and investing it into your game after just a few hours spent on a book, video, or course. This concept is life changing. Do not be a soccer player who slowly gets better; find a mentor who will allow you to jump the 10,000-hour learning curve.

Other loopholes to consider are learning how to become better from your coach(es) or parent(s). A coach can be a mentor, but more often than not, their focus is on many players on the team and not just your specific skills and abilities. **Coaches often focus on getting the team to work better and not necessarily on getting each individual player to become better themselves.**

Also, you can learn from a teammate who gives you advice after making a mistake. Most people are offended when others give them feedback and I will be honest and say I was like this for many years. However, it has been said, **"If you correct a fool, he will hate you; correct a wise man and he will love you."** I speak from experience when I say I was once a fool to feedback, but it is way more rewarding to be wise to feedback. As such, be the wise soccer player open to feedback from teammates, coaches, and parents.

Additionally, you are human and will make mistakes. **Therefore, it is a must that you are okay with making a mistake once but figuring out why you made it and how to correct it going forward.** Furthermore, you can watch other soccer players to learn from their success and mistakes. Watching the English Premier League, La Liga, Bundesliga, Serie A, Ligue 1, MLS, and even your own footage will help you see how the best players perform and where your game can be improved. Lastly, visualizing your skills and practicing them in your mind is nearly as effective as performing them on the field, so you can almost always find time to visualize even if you do not have time to make it to the soccer field to train.

In conclusion, the soccer learning curve can be steep. Find a mentor to help you on your journey to become a great soccer player. **A mentor is a great way to help you achieve your 10,000 hours in less time, so you can experience the success you have dreamed about.** Do not be a player who avoids this advice and watches their teammates and opponents become better than you more quickly.

Afterword

I hope you have learned how to open your mind to feedback from others, become okay with making mistakes, and view the game as a springboard to achieve your goals. Your attitude towards both soccer and the world will make a huge impact on your success. Having a positive attitude does not make a situation any easier. However, it does make the situation seem easier. Therefore, I challenge you to continue growing your knowledge of the game. Find at least one mentor to help you leap over your competition knowing that you do not need to make the mistakes yourself because you can learn from somebody else's mistakes.

Avoid the pain of missing out on the technology age we currently live in where access to resources and information on how to improve your soccer game is easily available and very affordable. Remember that changing/growing can be scary at times. However, it is much scarier to stay the same when everyone around you is becoming better. As a result, know that you are trading discomfort in the current moment for future success. If it seems like you are going through tough times, do not stop. Overcome the tough times so you can have the success you so badly desire on the other side. As the United States Women's Soccer Team's all-star forward, Alex Morgan, points out, "You are your biggest competition." **If you enjoyed this book, please leave a review on Amazon to let me know!**

WAIT!

Wouldn't it be nice to have an easy 1-page checklist of the steps to master your morning? Need the tasks to do to make sure you have a terrific start to your day? Well, here is your chance!

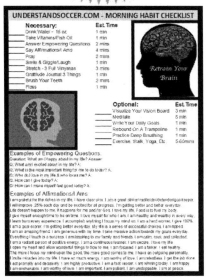

Go to this Link for an **Instant** 1-Page Printout:
UnderstandSoccer.com/free-printout

This FREE checklist is simply a "Thank You" for purchasing this book. This 1-page checklist will ensure that you take advantage of every morning to bring you closer to becoming the best soccer player you can be!

About the Author

There he was, a soccer player who had difficulties scoring. He wanted to be the best on the field but lacked the confidence and know-how to make his goal a reality. Every day, he dreamed about improving, but the average coaching and lack of knowledge only left him feeling alone and like he couldn't attain his goal. He was a quiet player and his performance often went unnoticed.

This all changed after his junior year on the Varsity soccer team of one of the largest high schools in the state. During the team and parent banquet at the end of the season, his coach decided to say something nice about each player. When it came to his turn to receive praise, the only thing that could be said was that he had scored two goals that season even though it was against a lousy team, so they didn't really count...

It was a very painful statement that after the 20+ game season, all that could be said of his efforts were two goals that didn't count. Since that moment, he has been forever changed considering one of his greatest fears came true; he was called out in front of his family and friends. Because of that, he got serious. With a new soccer mentor, he focused on the training necessary to obtain the skills to build his confidence and become the goal scorer he always dreamed of being. The next season, after just a few months, he found himself moved up to the starting position of center midfielder and scored his first goal of the 26-game season in only the third game.

He kept up the additional training led by a proven goal scorer to build his knowledge. Fast forward to present day and as a result of the work and focus on the necessary skills, he figured out how to become a goal scorer who averages about two goals and an assist per game, all because of an increase in his understanding of how to play soccer. With the help of a soccer mentor, he was able to take his game from bench-warmer who got called out in front of everybody to the most confident player on the field.

Currently, he is a soccer trainer in Michigan working for Next Level Training. He advanced through their rigorous program as a soccer player and was hired as a trainer. This program has allowed him to guide world-class soccer players for over a decade. He trains soccer players in formats ranging from one-hour classes to weeklong camps, and he instructs classes of all sizes, from groups of 30 soccer players all the way down to working one-on-one with individuals who are looking to play for the United States National Team. If you enjoy this book, please leave a review.

Additional Books by Dylan Joseph Available on Amazon:

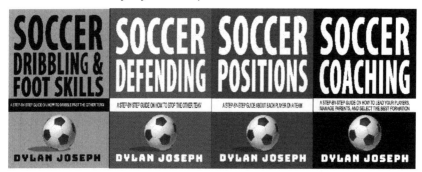

Soccer Dribbling & Foot Skills: A Step-by-Step Guide on How to Dribble Past the Other Team

Soccer Defending: A Step-by-Step Guide on How to Stop the Other Team

Soccer Positions: A Step-by-Step Guide about Each Player on a Team

Soccer Coaching: A Step-by-Step Guide on How to Lead Your Players, Manage Parents, and Select the Best Formation

Free Book!

How would you like to get a book of your choosing in the *Understand Soccer* series for free?

Join the Soccer Squad Book Team today and receive your next book (and potentially future books) for FREE.

Signing up is easy and does not cost anything.

Check out this website for more information:

UnderstandSoccer.com/soccer-squad-book-team

Thank You for Reading!

Dear Reader,

I hope you enjoyed and learned from **Soccer Mindset**. I truly enjoyed writing these steps and tips to ensure you feel confident in your thoughts.

As an author, I love feedback. Candidly, you are the reason that I wrote this book and plan to write more. Therefore, tell me what you liked, what you loved, and what can be improved. I'd love to hear from you. Visit UnderstandSoccer.com and scroll to the bottom of the homepage to leave me a message in the contact section or email me at:

Dylan@UnderstandSoccer.com

Finally, I need to ask a favor. **I'd love and truly appreciate a review.**

As you likely know, reviews are a key part of my process to see whether you, the reader, enjoyed my book. The reviews allow me to write more books. You have the power to help make or break my book. Please take the 2 minutes to leave a review on Amazon.com at:

https://www.amazon.com/gp/product-review/1949511197.

In gratitude,

Dylan Joseph

Appendix
Answer Key to Locus of Control Activity

External Locus of Control = **ELOC**

Internal Locus of Control = **ILOC**

A. It is too hard to be good at soccer these days. **(ELOC)**

B. I know it is up to me to become good at soccer. **(ILOC)**

A. Joining a good soccer team depends on me being in the right place at the right time and knowing the right people. **(ELOC)**

B. Becoming a success in soccer is a matter of hard work; luck has little or nothing to do with it. **(ILOC)**

A. What happens to me in soccer is my own doing. **(ILOC)**

B. Sometimes, I feel like I do not have enough control over the direction my soccer career is taking. **(ELOC)**

A. In the long run, people receive the respect they deserve in soccer. **(ILOC)**

B. Unfortunately, an individual's worth in soccer often passes unrecognized, no matter how hard they try. **(ELOC)**

A. The coach is the major factor in how well I play for a team. **(ELOC)**

B. I have the greatest control over how I play for a team. **(ILOC)**

A. Without the right breaks, one cannot be an effective coach of a soccer team. **(ELOC)**

B. Capable people who fail to become good coaches have not yet taken advantage of their opportunities. **(ILOC)**

A. Players who cannot get along with other players do not understand how to do so. **(ILOC)**

B. No matter how hard you try, some teammates will not like you. **(ELOC)**

A. When I make plans in soccer, I am almost always certain that I can make them work. **(ILOC)**

B. It is not always wise to plan too far ahead in soccer because many things turn out to be a matter of luck anyway. **(ELOC)**

Of the 8 statement pairings, how many external locus of control statements did you agree with? How many internal locus of control statements did you relate to? Although there are absolutely things outside your control, having a higher internal locus of control will allow you to have more confidence in your actions and an increased identity capital. It will provide you with the opportunity to ask better questions and find better answers to how you can travel from where you are to where you want to be. Believing that most of your life's circumstances are outside of your control often will lead you to not taking any action to change them. Hoping for luck is a tough thing to build a soccer career on. Instead, understand that the more you believe you can control, the more you will be able to change what you do not like and obtain more of what you enjoy.

Glossary

80/20 Principle - 80% of your results come from only 20% of your actions.

10,000 Hour Rule - It takes approximately 10,000 hours of deliberate practice to become an expert in a field.

Attacking Midfielder - A player positioned on the field between defenders and forwards and often get many assists by acting as the playmaker on the team to create scoring chances for other midfielders and forwards.

Attacking Touch - Pushing the ball into space with your first touch, which is the opposite of taking a touch where the ball stops underneath you (i.e., at your feet).

Attitude - A way of thinking or feeling about someone or something, typically one that is reflected in a person's behavior.

Bicycle Kick (i.e., "Overhead Kick") - Where you jump up and kick the ball while the ball is in the air above you.

Big 3 Foot Skills - The jab, la croqueta, and the shot fake.

Carbohydrates - Sugar, starch, and cellulose that typically can be broken down to release energy in the human body.

Challenging - Inviting competition to test one's abilities.

Champions League - The UEFA Champions League is an annual soccer competition involving the best club teams from many of the professional leagues in Europe to crown the European Club Champion. Often considered one of the top two trophies that every soccer player dreams of winning (the other being the World Cup).

Comfort Zone - A psychological state where things feel familiar to a person and they are at ease and in control of their environment while experiencing low levels of anxiety and stress but not growing.

Compliment - An expression of praise or admiration.

Compound Interest - The exact method of how interest is calculated in your savings account, which includes interest on principal and on other interest. With this book, it is how practicing skills can compound and be exponential.

Deliberate Practice - This form of practice is purposeful practice that knows where the player needs to go and how to get there. It is guided by an understanding of what expert performers do to excel. For example, juggling with the tops of your feet towards the toes 30 times in a row to become better at settling the ball out of the air.

Diminishing Return Learning Curve - A learning curve where the rate of increase in skill is higher in the beginning but decreases with time until it reaches zero additional skill for more added time, at which point the person has achieved the maximum skill. This type of learning curve is most common for non-complex tasks.

Dynamic Stretches - Active movements where joints and muscles go through a full range of motion and there are no static stretches being held. These stretches are functional and mimic the movements in soccer to help your body warm up for a game.

Empowering Questions - Open-ended questions that invite people to ponder, consider, notice, and discover things about themselves and the world around them. They create insights, "ah-ha" moments, and future opportunities.

External Locus of Control - Believing external circumstances like the weather, teammates' opinions, what past coaches have taught, etc. is what shapes your future.

Failure - Giving up after a mistake without learning and applying how to correct it.

Fear Zone - The zone outside of your comfort zone where you are the most vulnerable and have the lowest self-confidence because of everything that you need to learn.

Fixed Mindset - Believing your basic qualities of intelligence, talent, humor, athletic ability, etc. are fixed traits.

Fulfillment - Achieving something desired, promised, or predicted.

Futebol de Salão - Brazilian 5v5 soccer that is oftentimes played on a basketball court.

Future Truth - Statements that are not currently true but will become true in the future through belief and action in the present.

Gifted - Having exceptional talent or natural ability.

Gratitude Journaling - Writing at least three things you are grateful for each day.

Growth Mindset - Believing your basic qualities of intelligence, talent, humor, athletic ability, etc. are abilities you have developed over time using knowledge and hard work.

Growth Zone - Where your dreams in soccer become a reality. This zone allows you to be okay with making mistakes because you know that you will contribute to your team's success every single game. You experience some anxiety in this zone but can turn it into motivation and fuel for productivity.

Habitual/Regular Practice - The most common form of practice where a person goes through the motions, repeating what they normally do, without being challenged or having a set goal. For example, practicing shooting from the penalty spot for the fifth practice in a row.

I Am - Most statements you attach to the words "I am" often become true in your life.

Identity Capital - Belief in who you are as a person and your ability to decide things for yourself.

Identity Crisis - A period of uncertainty and confusion in which a person's sense of identity becomes insecure, typically due to a change in their expected aims or role on a soccer team or in life.

Increasing Return Learning Curve - A learning curve where the more time spent learning makes it easier to learn more things. For example, a soccer player is acquiring skills, speed, and strength at an ever-increasing rate during their competitive career. This type of learning curve is most common for complex tasks.

Internal Locus of Control - Believing your own work ethic, perseverance, mindset, attitude, and feelings are ultimately what determine your future.

Learning Curve - Describes how much time is needed to master something.

Learning Zone - The zone after the fear zone where you will pick up the skills and abilities needed to overcome your problems and challenges. This zone requires work but is the last step before achieving your goal in the growth zone.

Locus of Control - How much a person believes they can control the outcomes of events in their lives.

Loss Prevention - Taking measures to prevent losing which often detracts from focusing on winning.

Meditation - Thinking deeply or focusing your mind for a period of time, in silence for spiritual purposes or as a method of relaxation.

Mentor - An experienced and trusted adviser who can take their experiences and direct you on how to achieve your goals and dreams much more quickly.

Mindset - The established set of attitudes and beliefs held by someone.

Mistake - A wrong action.

Never Miss A Cone - The idea that skills compound so missing cones in practice limits the number of opportunities you have to get better.

Opposite Foot - Your non-dominant foot. Out of your two feet, it is the one you are not as comfortable using.

Panic Zone - Burning out and distance yourself from learning new skills because you try to take on too much at once. In this zone, you will find yourself not being as excited about soccer as you are when you learn just one thing in-depth at a time.

Parenting - Raising a child.

Process Behaviors - What a soccer player has control over and can perform regardless of how the game is unfolding. Things like being aggressive, playing hard, staying level-headed, keeping your head up, having fun, communicating, and being positive with yourself and teammates.

Psychology - The scientific study of the human mind and its functions, especially those affecting behavior in a given circumstance.

Purposeful Practice - Practice where you set specific goals for what you want to complete successfully. For example, I want to juggle the ball 30 times without letting it hit the ground.

Reframing - A way of viewing and experiencing events, ideas, concepts, and emotions to find more positive alternatives.

S.M.A.R.T Goal - Setting a goal that is specific, measurable, attainable, relevant, and timely.

Sandwich Feedback Technique - Giving a compliment, then providing constructive feedback, and finishing with another compliment to ensure someone hears your words but does not resent your feedback.

Scissor - When the foot closest to the ball goes around the ball as you are attempting to dribble an opposing player. Emphasize turning your hips to fake the defender by planting past the ball with your foot that is not going around the ball, so you can use the momentum of the moving ball to your advantage.

Shot Fake - Faking a shot. Make sure your form looks the same as when you shoot, including: 1) Looking at the goal before you do a shot fake 2) Arms out 3) Raise your shooting leg high enough behind your body, so it looks like you are going to shoot.

Silver Lining - Finding a positive aspect in something negative.

Simple Interest - The quick and rough method of calculating interest in your savings account, which only has the interest on the principal. With this book, it is how players view practicing skills as additive even though building abilities is exponential (as shown through compound interest).

Subconscious Mind - An unquestioning servant that works day and night to make sure your behavior fits a pattern consistent with your emotionalized thoughts, hopes, beliefs and desires.

Synovial Fluids - A fluid found in the cavities of joints that reduces friction between the cartilage of the joints during movement.

Talent - Naturally have the skill, gifts, and aptitude.

Threatening - Causing someone to feel vulnerable or at risk.

Vision Board - A tool used to help clarify, concentrate, and focus on life goals. It is any board on which you display images that represent whatever you want to be, do, or have in your life.

Visualization - Mentally rehearsing the game situations you are likely to come across to ensure you know how you will react.

Winger - Playing in the flanks, these attackers' opposition are usually the other team's full backs. Their role is like that of outside midfielders, except these attackers play farther up the field and are expected to score significantly more than outside midfielders.

Acknowledgments

I would like to thank you, the reader. I am grateful to provide you value and to help you on your journey of becoming a more confident and tougher soccer player. I am happy to serve you and thank you for the opportunity to do so. Also, I would like to recognize people that have made a difference and have paved the way for me to share this book with you:

I want to thank the grammar editor Abbey Decker. Her terrific understanding of the complexities of the English language ensured that the wording needed to convey the messages was appropriate and she provided countless grammatical improvements.

Also, I would like to thank the content editors Kevin Solorio, Michael Mroczka, Toni Sinistaj, and Youssef Hodroj. They reviewed this book for areas that could be improved and additional insights to share that could immediately help you, the reader.

Many thanks,

Dylan Joseph

Made in the USA
Middletown, DE
13 October 2022